Twayne's English Authors Series

EDITOR OF THIS VOLUME

Bertram H. Davis

Florida State University

Dr. John Arbuthnot

TEAS 256

John Arbuthnot, M.D.

DR. JOHN ARBUTHNOT

By ROBERT C. STEENSMA

University of Utah

TWAYNE PUBLISHERS

A DIVISION OF G. K. HALL & CO., BOSTON

Library of Congress Cataloging in Publication Data

Steensma, Robert.
Dr. John Arbuthnot.

(Twayne's English authors series ; TEAS 256)
Bibliography: p.   137 - 43
Includes
1.   Arbuthnot, John, 1667 - 1735—
Criticism and interpretation.   I.   Title
PR3316.A5Z87   828'.5'09   78-24237
ISBN 0-8057-6749-5

For my mother and father,
Martha and Tony Steensma

Contents

About the Author

Robert C. Steensma, Professor of English at the University of Utah, received his B.A. from Augustana College (South Dakota), his M.A. from the University of South Dakota, and his Ph.D. from the University of Kentucky.

He has taught at Augustana, the University of South Dakota, Utah State University, and, as a Fulbright lecturer, the University of Jÿvaskÿla in Finland.

Among his publications are a previous Twayne book on Sir William Temple and articles on Temple, Jonathan Swift, Walt Whitman, Ben Jonson, Daniel Defoe, Restoration drama, western American literature, and American naval history. He has published in such journals as *Shakespeare Newsletter, College English, Rocky Mountain Review, Naval Institute Proceedings, Naval War College Review, Western Humanities Review, Notes and Queries, Walt Whitman Review,* and *Neuphilologische Mitteilungen.*

He is a Captain in the U. S. Naval Reserve and is currently assigned to NATO.

Preface

Samuel Johnson called him the most eminent man in the reign of Queen Anne; Jonathan Swift thought him "a perfectly honest man"; and Alexander Pope memorialized him in his most personal poem as "Friend to my Life." And yet Dr. John Arbuthnot today somehow remains on the periphery of early eighteenth-century English literature, largely because of his self-effacing personality and his reluctance to translate his satiric wit and intellectual agility into the kind of enduring literary work that keeps his friends such as Pope, Swift, William Congreve, and John Gay in the forefront of our concern with the first half of the eighteenth century. One of his works—*The History of John Bull,* which satirized the most divisive war in English history and gave the English spirit its famous personification—is read today only by specialists and is accessible to the general reader only in expensive or scarce editions. His other major work (though some of it may be by other hands) is *The Memoirs of Martinus Scriblerus,* which satirizes corruptions in learning; it, too, is scarce and is studied mainly in terms of its relationship to the work of his friends in the Scriblerus circle. His other works are scattered through a variety of eighteenth-century collections, including those of his friends, and there is in print no modern or reliable edition of his complete works.

But to his contemporaries—people as diverse in personality and achievement as Pope, Swift, Gay, Congreve, the Duchess of Marlborough, and Queen Anne herself—Arbuthnot was known not only as a trusted friend and wise physician, but also as a versatile scientist, a lively wit, an amusing and clever writer, and a gentle man. Coming up to London about 1691 as a young teacher of mathematics, Arbuthnot went on to become a doctor of medicine, an amateur numismatist and geologist, and a writer who could turn out readable and expert treatises on such varied topics as smallpox, coins, weights and measures, geology, and mathematics, and sparkling satires on prevailing fopperies, political chicanery, and pedantry.

Such a man, quietly pursuing his profession amid the intrigues of court and ministry, cherishing his friendships with many of the political and literary notables of the age without incurring any notable enemies, enjoying his children and his card games, and tending to the needs of his family, deserves more attention than he has hitherto been given. One might, indeed, learn as much about the early eighteenth century in England from a reading of Arbuthnot's work as he would from a study of the doctor's better-known contemporaries, for in his writings we find many of the same intellectual, political, and social problems which concerned Swift, Pope, and Gay.

The purpose of my study is to examine Arbuthnot's life and work against the backdrop of the reign of Queen Anne (1702 - 1714), but the discussion will necessarily extend into the period of the two Georges until 1735, the year of Arbuthnot's death. My focus will be primarily on his literary work, but such an analysis would be incomplete without reference to his efforts in other disciplines. Thus, after reviewing his life and career in Chapter 1, I will move on in subsequent chapters to his satires and his scientific writings (for a more detailed discussion of Arbuthnot's work in science, the student will be well repaid for consulting Lester M. Beattie's *John Arbuthnot, Mathematician and Satirist*, which after forty years remains the fullest and best book on the man and his work). Because so little of Arbuthnot's writing is readily available to modern readers, I have taken the liberty of quoting more copiously from his works to demonstrate style and substance than would be either necessary or wise in the case of a better-known and better-edited figure. Such a survey, I hope, will contribute to a better understanding of Arbuthnot and his work, and also encourage other scholars to turn their attention to broader and deeper studies of the man and his career. The books by Beattie and George Aitken, as well as the handful of articles and dissertations, still leave unexplored areas of Arbuthnot's life and writings that we need to know more about.

In the course of writing this book I have incurred a number of personal and scholarly debts. To Sylvia Bowman, founder of this series, I wish to express my thanks for her patience and editorial counsel. I also wish to thank Diane Elwood Hall for valuable research and typing assistance in the early stages of this work, Milton Voigt and William R. Slager (successive heads of my department) for research funds and logistic support, and Joyce Sorrell, Karen Anastasopoulos, and Mei Wang for several thoughtful courtesies. The members of my graduate seminar in the Scriblerus Club at the University of Utah in the spring of 1972—Rosemary Beless, Les Emmett, Phil Hansen, Mary Hewes, and Doris Paul—contributed helpful ideas and challenged some of mine, as did David Lee in another seminar. Mohammad Habib assisted me in tracking down certain bibliographical items. Beth Burdett, a valued colleague, located copies of several works and annotated them in the British Museum. The librarians at the University of Utah, Utah State University, the University of Texas, and Cambridge University were also helpful.

Sharon, Mike, Laura, Kathryn, and Rebecca also deserve a special acknowledgment, as does David Moore, an engineer and best of friends, who gave me a patient listening and raised certain hard—and sensible—questions that would never occur to a college professor.

Chronology

1667	John Arbuthnot born in the parish of Arbuthnott, Scotland, and baptized on April 29, the eldest of eight children of the Reverend Alexander Arbuthnott, an Anglican clergyman, and Margaret Lammy Arbuthnott. "Arbuthnott" was the traditonal family spelling after the mid-seventeenth century, but "Arbuthnot" was used by the doctor on the title pages of his works and by his contemporaries.
1681(?)	Enters Marischal College, Aberdeen.
1685	Receives Master of Arts at Marischal.
1691	Spring, death of father.
1691(?)	Goes to London to teach mathematics.
1692	Publishes first book, *Of the Laws of Chance*, anonymously at London.
1694	Enters University College, Oxford, as a fellow-commoner.
1696	September, receives Doctor of Medicine degree by examination from St. Andrews.
1697	December, publishes *An Examination of Dr. Woodward's Account of the Deluge.*
1701	Publishes *An Essay on the Usefulness of Mathematical Learning.*
1703	Birth of son George.
1704	Elected Fellow of the Royal Society on St. Andrews Day, November 24.
1705	Birth of son Charles. Summer, publishes *Tables of the Grecian, Roman and Jewish Measures, Weights and Coins;* October 30, appointed Physician Extraordinary to the Queen.
1706	Publishes *A Sermon Preach'd to the People at Mercat-Cross* on the subject of the pending union of England and Scotland.
1709	Appointed Physician Ordinary to Queen Anne in November as a consequence of his eminent medical services to the royal family.

1710   April 27, admitted as a Fellow of the Royal Society of Physicians; publishes *An Argument for Divine Providence* in the *Philosophical Transactions* of the Royal Society.

1711(?)   Appointed to a post in the Customs; probably meets Jonathan Swift for the first time.

1712   March, publication of *Law is a Bottomless-Pit*, the first of the *John Bull* pamphlets, followed in the same month by *John Bull in His Senses*, in May by *An Appendix to John Bull Still in His Senses*, and in July by *Lewis Baboon Turned Honest, and John Bull Politician* (all reprinted in 1727 as *The History of John Bull*); October, *The Art of Political Lying* published.

1713   Appointed Physician at Chelsea Hospital. March 31, Treaty of Utrecht ends the War of the Spanish Succession (begun 1701). Spring, gives Robert Harley, first Earl of Oxford and coleader of the Tory ministry, memorandum "Concerning the Peace" as strategy to counter Whig opposition to the Treaty of Utrecht.

1713 - 1714   Winter and spring, meetings of the Scriblerus Club—Arbuthnot, Gay, Thomas Parnell, Pope, Swift, and occasionally others—which eventuates in *The Memoirs of Martinus Scriblerus*.

1714   August 1, death of Queen Anne and fall of Tories, including Swift and Arbuthnot, who loses his royal appointments, briefly visits his brother Robert in Paris, and takes a house in Dover Street, Piccadilly.

1715   Brothers George and Robert involved in Jacobite plot to invade England, Robert (a banker) by conveying £5,000 - 10,000 from the Duke of Marlborough to Prince James (the "Pretender") in France.

1716   Publishes *The Humble Petition of the Colliers*, a satire.

1717   Collaborates with Gay and Pope on *Three Hours after Marriage*, a comedy which opens on January 16 and fails after seven nights.

1718   Journey of several months to France with six weeks each at Paris and Rouen, visiting Robert Arbuthnot and other Jacobites.

1719   Controversy over smallpox involving Doctors John Freind, John Woodward, Richard Mead, Sir Richard Steele, and Arbuthnot.

1723 Appointed Second Censor by the Royal College of Physicians.

1724 *The Quidnuncki's* and *Reasons Humbly Offered by the Upholders,* both satires, published.

1727 *Tables of Ancient Coins, Weights and Measures* published; Swift and Pope's *Miscellanies in Verse and Prose* appears, containing *The History of John Bull* and *The Art of Political Lying.* October 5, chosen an Elect by the College of Physicians; October 18, delivers the Harvaean Oration, which is published shortly afterward.

1728 - Moves to Cork Street in Burlington Gardens, his home
1729(?) for the remainder of his life.

1729 *Virgilius Restauratus* printed as an appendix to Pope's *Dunciad Variorum.* October, wife, Margaret, near death.

1730 Death of Margaret of apoplexy on May 3.

1731 February, publication of *A Brief Account of Mr. Ginglicutt's Treatise* (a satire); May, *An Essay Concerning the Nature of Aliments* printed. Death of son Charles on December 2.

1732 "An Epitaph on Francis Charteris" printed in April in the *London Magazine* and the *Gentleman's Magazine. An Essay Concerning the Origin of the Sciences,* a satire, published in Volume III of the Pope-Swift *Miscellanies.* December 4, death of Gay.

1733 July, *An Essay Concerning the Effects of Air on Human Bodies* published.

1734 *Know Yourself,* a philosophic poem, published; summer, moves to Hampstead temporarily as health fails.

1735 Pope publishes his *Epistle of Dr. Arbuthnot* in January. February 27, death of Arbuthnot at age sixty-seven in Cork Street home; buried in St. James's Church, Piccadilly, on March 4.

1740 Death of daughter Margaret.

1744 Death of Pope on May 30.

1745 Swift dies on October 19.

1751 Death of daughter Anne; first collected (but unauthorized) edition of Arbuthnot's works.

1779 Death of son George, thus ending the direct line of Dr. Arbuthnot.

CHAPTER 1

"A Perfectly Honest Man"

WHEN young John Arbuthnot, in his mid-twenties, arrived in London about 1691 with a Master of Arts degree from Marischal College, Aberdeen, and no encouraging prospects, he entered an exciting social and literary world in which he was to move for over four decades until his death in 1735. The intellectual atmosphere was alive with discussion of John Locke's *Two Treatises of Government* and *An Essay Concerning Human Understanding*, both published in 1690, and Isaac Newton's *Philosophiae Naturalis Principia Mathematica* was the talk of the scientists. Politically, Englishmen were several years into a war against Europe's archvillain, Louis XIV of France, a struggle which presaged the even longer war which would begin in 1701 and continue until 1713, when Arbuthnot would become famous as the author of the *John Bull* pamphlets. In 1691 John Dryden, nearing the end of his long and productive career, produced his opera *King Arthur,* and in the same year George Etherege, one of the leading Restoration playwrights, went to his grave, as did two eminent divines, the Quaker George Fox and the Presbyterian Richard Baxter.

Thus Arbuthnot came up to London just as the older generation of Restoration notables was passing into eclipse and as his own was moving toward its place in the sun. Jonathan Swift, born in the same year (1667) as Arbuthnot, was returning from Ireland to resume his work at Moor Park with the aging diplomat and essayist Sir William Temple. Joseph Addison and Richard Steele were still at Oxford, the first taking his degree and the latter moving through his studies at Christ Church and Merton. William Congreve, only a few years removed from Trinity College, Dublin, was ready (in 1692) to publish his slight and only novel, *Incognita*, before producing his first play, *The Old Bachelor*, at the theater in Drury Lane in 1693. But among the others whose circle of friendship and collaboration Arbuthnot was later to enter, Alexander Pope was three years old

and John Gay six. Daniel Defoe, the Dissenter and never the intimate of these men, was going bankrupt in the amount of seventeen thousand pounds. For the next forty years these were the men
who not only produced the plays, poems, pamphlets, and books
which were to dominate the shelves of the booksellers, but also
assumed an active and influential role in English political and intellectual affairs in the reigns of Mary and the first two Georges.

I *Physician and Wit*

John Arbuthnot was born in the Scottish parish of Arbuthnott
(the traditional spelling), Kincardineshire, in late April 1667 and
was baptized on the twenty-ninth of that month, the eldest of eight
children born to the Reverend Alexander Arbuthnott and his wife,
Margaret. The elder Arbuthnott, an Anglican clergyman, was later
to be deprived of his living in 1689 when he refused to subscribe to
the official restoration of Presbyterianism in Scotland, and upon his
death in 1691 burial of his corpse was delayed until the Session
Book he had taken with him into retirement was surrendered to the
kirk session by young John.[1] This treatment of his father may well
have influenced Arbuthnot's aversion to religious factionalism and
to Scots Presbyterianism as well.

Unfortunately, little else is known of the first thirty years of Arbuthnot's life other than that he took his master's degree at
Marischal College in 1685, lived in London (perhaps with William
Pate, a woolen-draper) while teaching mathematics, became a
fellow-commoner at Oxford in 1694, received his Doctor of
Medicine degree by examination from St. Andrews in 1696, and
started his medical practice.[2] During this period he probably began
his career as a writer; a short book, *Of the Laws of Chance*, the first
of his numerous works on science and mathematics, appeared at
London in 1692. The book is by no means a major work or an
original one (in the preface Arbuthnot admits that it is for the most
part a translation of Christiaan Huygens's *De ratiociniis in ludo
Aleae*), but it anticipates his later mathematical studies in *An Essay
on the Usefulness of Mathematical Learning* (1701) and *An Argument for Divine Providence* (1710).

After 1696 his trail is much easier to follow as he became increasingly involved and well known in London, first as a physician
and later as an intimate of Swift and Pope. From 1697 to 1711,
when he probably first met Swift, he was busy establishing his prac-

tice, marrying Margaret, and fathering two sons, George and Charles, in 1703 and 1705 (there were other children who did not survive to maturity); and continuing his writing on various non-literary subjects (*An Examination of Dr. Woodward's Account of the Deluge*, 1697; *An Essay on the Usefulness of Mathematical Learning*, 1701; *Tables of the Grecian, Roman and Jewish Measures, Weights and Coins*, 1706; and *An Argument for Divine Providence*, 1710). He was also advancing his medical career by becoming a fellow of the Royal Society in 1704, Physician Extraordinary to Queen Anne the next year and her Physician Ordinary in 1709, and a fellow of the Royal College of Physicians in 1710. His service to the royal family had begun several years earlier when he treated Prince George, who had become unexpectedly and seriously ill.

Nothing to this point in his career seemed to anticipate the gently satiric genius shortly to emerge in the *John Bull* pamphlets and his collaboration with the members of the Scriblerus Club.

The year 1711 might well be looked upon as the turning point of Arbuthnot's career, for in this year he probably met Jonathan Swift for the first time and began a friendship which would endure for almost a quarter of a century. His friendship with Swift brought Arbuthnot into the circle of Tory wits who founded the Scriblerus Club several years later and watched with increasing despair and frustration the decline and fall of the Tory ministry of Harley and Bolingbroke which had brought an end to the long and divisive War of the Spanish Succession with the Treaty of Utrecht in 1713. But these clouds lay in the distance when Swift wrote, on March 19, 1710 - 1711, of a new acquaintance to Esther Johnson, his beloved "Stella": "The Duke of Argyle is gone; and whether he has my memorial, I know not, till I see Dr. Arbuthnot, to whom I gave it. That hard name belongs to a Scotch doctor, an acquaintance of the duke's and me; Stella can't pronounce it."[3]

Within five months the men were on intimate terms, as we see in another of Swift's letters to Stella: "Dr. Arbuthnott, the queen's physician and favourite, went out with me to shew me the places: we went a little after the queen, and overtook Miss Forester, a maid of honour, on her palfry taking the air; we made her go along with us. We saw the place they have made for a famous horse-race tomorrow, where the queen will come. We met the queen coming back, and Miss Forester stood, like us, with her hat off while the queen went by. The Dr. and I left the lady where we found her, but under other conductors, and we dined at a little place he has taken, about a mile off."[4]

Although the first extant correspondence between the two men is not dated earlier than June 12 and 16, 1714,[5] they were undoubtedly drawn together by their political and literary interests, an intimacy which would continue through Swift's last letter to his friend in November 1734, only a few months before Arbuthnot's death. The quality of their relationship over several decades is indicated in Swift's letter to Erasmus Lewis on July 23, 1737, two years after his friend's passing: "I have found my share of affliction sufficient, in the loss of Dr. Arbuthnot, and poor Gay, and others."[6] But perhaps Swift's finest tribute to Arbuthnot is found in his "Verses on the Death of Dr. Swift," published in 1731:

> ARBUTHNOT is no more my friend,
> Who dares to Irony pretend;
> Which I was born to introduce,
> Refin'd it first, and shew'd its Use.[7]

Swift, like others, admired Arbuthnot for his satirical talents and intellectual brilliance as well as for his amiability and gentle nature.

In the meantime Arbuthnot's duties as physician to the queen were increasingly taking up his time as her health declined toward her eventual death in 1714. As early as September 1711 Arbuthnot was treating her for the gout at Windsor;[8] he ministered to her again at Windsor in September 1712 and March 1714, and during her terminal illness before her death at 7:00 a.m. on August 1.[9] His duties at Court, however, were not simply those of a royal physician, for he found himself, perhaps reluctantly, drawn into the intrigues of the Whigs and Tories in the last years of Anne's reign regarding the controversial Treaty of Utrecht and the choice of a successor to the childless queen. He remained loyal to the memory of the queen and to her Hanoverian successor, George I, though his brothers, George and Robert, were strongly (and correctly) suspected of Jacobitism in working for the restoration of the Stuart line.[10] After Anne's death his duties at court ceased, though he remained on good terms with the royal family.[11]

During these difficult years Arbuthnot continued to expand his activities and acquaintances. In 1712 he served on a committee of the Royal Society to decide the dispute between the followers of Sir Isaac Newton and Gottfried Wilhelm Leibniz as to which eminent mathematician first invented infinitesimal calculus; the committee's decision (probably not without nationalistic bias) was ultimately rendered in favor of Newton.[12] This was Arbuthnot's second period of service to the Society; previously, in 1705, he had worked on another committee with Newton, Sir Christopher Wren, and others to supervise the printing of the star catalogues of John Flamsteed, the Astronomer Royal, which were not published until 1712 and then only after a long and rancorous quarrel involving Flamsteed, the committee, and Edmund Halley, a controversy from which Arbuthnot himself did not emerge unscathed.[13]

The year 1712 also saw the emergence of Arbuthnot as a satirist in a series of pamphlets later reprinted in 1727 as *The History of John Bull*. The *John Bull* pamphlets mark the his first appearance as an imaginative writer and probably did much to make him known to the literary public and establish his reputation. More will be said later of these five pamphlets, but it is sufficient for now to point out that the satires had their inspiration and genesis in the controversy surrounding the attempts of the Tory ministry of Robert Harley and Henry St. John (Bolingbroke) to bring to an end the long War of the Spanish Succession with France and Louis XIV which had raged on the Continent since 1701. Although the war had witnessed the great victories of John Churchill, Duke of Marlborough, the darling of the Whigs, at Blenheim (1704), Ramillies (1706), Oudenarde (1708), and Malplaquet (1709), it had divided the English public as badly as the Vietnam War did the American public in the late 1960s and early 1970s. The Whigs, who had refused Louis's peace offer in 1709, seemed to be less eager than the Tories to end the war (because they were profiting from it, some opponents believed). When the Tories, came to power in 1710, they vowed to end it quickly, partly because some of them believed they were paying most of the taxes necessary to its continuation.

In defending the Tory peace policy, Arbuthnot developed a political allegory in which John Bull (England) and Nicholas Frog (Holland) engaged in a lawsuit against Lewis Baboon (Louis XIV), employ Hocus (Marlborough) as their attorney, and finally gain possession of Ecclesdown (Dunkirk) after a meeting at Salutation Tavern (the Congress of Utrecht). The complete satire, occasional in nature and replete with now-dim historical and political allusions, is pointed, robust, and amusing, all the more so in the light of the peace treaty signed at Utrecht in 1713.

Later in the year (October) Arbuthnot continued his attack on the

Whigs with a short satirical piece, *The Art of Political Lying*, in which he assumes the persona of an abstractor who summarizes the contents of the first volume of a forthcoming treatise on political deceit. The persona pretends to be objective and nonpartisan, but throughout the ironically detached discussion of the art of lying is an implicit accusation that the Whigs are the most obvious exemplars and most astute practitioners of the venerable technique. Like the *John Bull* pamphlets, *The Art of Political Lying* shows Arbuthnot at his satiric best—whimsical, forceful, and witty. Surprisingly, it still reads well today.

Arbuthnot's success as a satirist in 1712 might account for his introduction to Alexander Pope and John Gay the next year. By this time Pope was already an accomplished poet, having produced his *Pastorals* (1709), *An Essay on Criticism* (1711), and the first version of *The Rape of the Lock* (1712)—notable achievements for a young man of twenty-four—and starting to accumulate a number of literary enemies. But Gay, now twenty-eight, had written his first play, *The Mohocks* (1712), and was to see his next, *The Wife of Bath*, produced at Drury Lane and his georgic *Rural Sports* published in 1713. His major works—*Trivia, The Shepherd's Week*, and *The Beggar's Opera*—were still to come.

Within a few months Arbuthnot was engaged in the satiric projects of the Scriblerus Club, an informal grouping which included not only Gay, Pope, Thomas Parnell, and Swift, but also occasionally Robert Harley (now Earl of Oxford), Bishop Francis Atterbury, and Congreve.[14] According to Pope, the group decided to ridicule "all the false tastes in learning, under the character of a man of capacity enough; that had dipped into every art and science, but injudiciously in each."[15] The project was dropped in 1714, when the club dispersed, and only the first book of *The Memoirs of Martinus Scriblerus* ever appeared in print, and then not until 1741 in the *Works* of Pope.

Arbuthnot's role in the authorship of the Scriblerus papers, to be discussed later at some length, was immense, and he was undoubtedly the guiding genius of the work, doing much of the writing and supplying much of the satire on education, music, logic, metaphysics, and science. Swift was probably correct in his estimate his influence on the project when he wrote to Arbuthnot on July 3, 1714: "To talk of Martin in any hands but yours, is a Folly. You every day give better hints than all of us together could do in a twelvemonth; And to say the Truth, Pope who first thought of the

Hint has no Genius at all to it, in my Mind. Gay is too young; Parnel has some Ideas of it, but is idle; I could putt together, and lard, and strike out well enough, but all that relates to the Sciences must be from you."[16] Influenced by a variety of earlier English and Continental literary traditions, the *Memoirs* were to prove significant in the evolution of Swift's *Gulliver's Travels* (1726) and Pope's *Dunciad* (1728), as well as some of their minor works.

After the death of Queen Anne, the fall of the Tory ministry, and the end of the Scriblerus Club (all in 1714), Arbuthnot's life remained comparatively placid and uneventful, though not without occasionally serious illness and heartache. In 1714 he moved to a house in Piccadilly and visited his brother Robert, a banker at Rouen, in Paris, as he was to do again in 1718. The next year two of his brothers, Robert and George, were deeply involved in plotting the invasion of England by the Old Pretender, James Francis Edward Stuart, son of James II (deposed in 1688), but neither was ever brought to justice.

In 1716 Arbuthnot again appeared in print with *The Humble Petition of the Colliers*, a *jeu d'esprit* in which colliers, cooks, blacksmiths, and others protest the proposals of projectors for providing all necessary kitchen fires by means of sunbeams and magnifying glasses. The following year Arbuthnot collaborated with Gay and Pope in the production of a comedy, *Three Hours after Marriage*, at Drury Lane on January 16. The play is a coarse and rollicking satire upon Dr. John Woodward (as Dr. Fossile), fellow of the Royal Society and eminent antiquarian at Gresham College, as well as upon the crusty critic John Dennis (as Sir Tremendous) and others. Arbuthnot's precise role in the writing of the play has never been determined (and probably never will be), nor has Pope's, but it seems certain that the largest share of the work was Gay's. At any rate, neither Arbuthnot nor Pope ever again wrote for the stage.

As we have seen, Arbuthnot had earlier published a number of scientific treatises, and in 1719 he may have become involved in a medical debate concerning cures for smallpox, a scholarly conflict which also brought forward contributions from Doctors John Freind, Richard Mead, John Woodward, and Sir Richard Steele. Freind had published two books of Hippocrates and appended a commentary on fevers in which he recommended purgation as a cure for the smallpox, but was challenged by Arbuthnot's old opponent, John Woodward, who advocated instead the use of emetics. Arbuthnot possibly wrote two attacks on Woodward's theory in

1719, *An Account of the Sickness and Death of Dr. W-dw-d* and
The Life and Adventures of Don Bilioso de l'Estomac. Although
both are somewhat characteristic of Arbuthnot, they are so tinged
with coarseness and there is so little evidence of his authorship that
modern scholars are reluctant to assign them to him.[17] In June the
quarrel assumed comic proportions as Woodward and Mead scuffl-
ed outside Gresham College, and the controversy continued for
some years.

Arbuthnot's private and public lives continued serenely for
several years. In 1723 he was appointed Second Censor of the Royal
College of Physicians; in 1724 he published *The Quidnuncki's* and
Reasons Humbly Offered by the Upholders, the first a poetical
satire upon political rumor-mongering which clearly demonstrates
that Arbuthnot's talents lay in prose rather than poetry, the second
a satire upon the apothecaries who were protesting a bill introduced
in Parliament by the physicians to forbid the dispensing of
medicines by apothecaries without prescription.

His old friendships continued on intimate terms, though Swift
was in Ireland. Pope, writing to Gay on September 11, 1722, comments on Arbuthnot's reluctance to acknowledge his authorship and
on his sociability:

Dr. *Arbuthnot* is a strange creature; he goes out of town, and leaves his
Bastards at other folks doors. I have long been so far mistaken in him as to
think him a Man of Morals as well as of Politicks. Pray let him know I made
a very unfashionable inquiry t'other day of the welfare of his Wife and
family: Things that (I presume) are below the consideration of a Wit and an
Ombre-player.[18]

And Arbuthnot, according to Pope (writing to John Caryll on
December 12, 1720), was not without his social consciousness; the
good doctor saw through the chicanery of the famous South Sea
scheme, an attempt on the part of the government to retire the
national debt by a rather dubious financial method which
bankrupted many speculators, including Gay. Pope reports that Arbuthnot

says the Government and South Sea Company only have locked up the
money of the people, upon conviction of their lunacy (as is usual in the case
of lunatics), and intend to restore 'em as much as is fit for such people, as
they see 'em return more and more to their senses.[19]

The resultant financial crash brought Sir Robert Walpole, the enemy of such literary men as Pope, Swift, and Henry Fielding, to power for two decades as one of England's greatest prime ministers. But in the autumn of 1725 Arbuthnot became critically ill. According to Pope, in a letter of September 14 to Swift, the cause of the ailment was an impostume (abscess) of the bowels;[20] and Gay, writing to William Fortescue on September 23, reports: "Dr. Arbuthnot has been at the point of death by a severe fit of illness, an imposthumation in the bowels; it hath broke, and he is now pretty well recovered."[21] Earlier, in October 1711, Arbuthnot had been seriously ill, but we know nothing of the nature of his sickness.

During the next five years or so Arbuthnot was occupied with more writing and with the anxieties attendant to illnesses and deaths within the circle of his family and literary friends. His next publication was the *Tables of Ancient Coins, Weights and Measures* (1727), an expansion of his work of 1705, a book which by modern standards has little value.[22] And in the same year appeared the Swift and Pope *Miscellanies,* published by Benjamin Motte, which brought together the five *John Bull* pamphlets into *The History of John Bull* and reprinted *The Art of Political Lying.* In 1729 a parody entitled *Virgilius Restauratus,* mocking Dr. Richard Bentley's classical scholarship on Terence, most probably by Arbuthnot, saw print in the variorum edition of Pope's *Dunciad.*

Arbuthnot, however, now in his mid-sixties, was beginning to feel the cold hand of mortality. In October 1729 his wife, Margaret, fell critically ill; she died of apoplexy on Sunday, May 3, 1730, and was buried in the Church of St. James's, Piccadilly, where Arbuthnot himself was to be interred five years later. Also in 1729 he lost two sisters-in-law. The sorrows of family losses were compounded by the deaths of Congreve in 1729 and Gay in late 1732. Swift, his closest friend, was back in Ireland, having made his last visit to England in 1727. His personal grief was intensified by the death of his son Charles on December 2, 1731, leaving him only his other son, George (who was to live until 1779), and his daughter Anne, who was to die unmarried at an unknown date.

But losses among family and friends did not paralyze Arbuthnot's spirit or creativity. In 1730 he is reported to have flogged a literary hack, James Moore-Smyth, for libelous comments in the latter's *One Epistle to Mr. Alexander Pope,*[23] and he continued to write and publish: *A Brief Account of Mr. John Ginglicutt's Treatise,* a satire upon political vilification (1731); the bitter and Juvenalian *Epitaph on Francis Charteris* (1732); *An Essay Concerning the Origin of the Sciences*, which continues the Scriblerian satire of pedantry (1732); *An Essay Concerning the Effects of Air on Human Bodies* (1733); and *Know Youself: A Poem* (1734).

In 1734 Arbuthnot's health again began to fail, and in the summer he moved to Hampstead. Bolingbroke, an old friend from the Scriblerian days, wrote to him sympathetically in July: "The bad state of yr health I lament with all my heart. God restore it, if ye order of his providence yt may be. I make you no compliment, I speak as I think; every man of virtue and sense like you, who goes off ye stage att this time, is an irreparable loss to our unhappy country. . . ."[24] By July 17 the old physician, writing to Pope, seemed to welcome death: "A Recovery in my Case, and at my Age, is impossible; the kindest Wish of my Friends is *Euthanasia.*"[25] In October he wrote to Swift in a similar vein: "I am afraid My dear freind we shall never see another more in this world. I shall to the last moment preserve my love & esteem for yow being well assured you will never leave the paths of virtue & honor for all that is in this world is not worth the least deviation from that way."[26] And one of his last letters (to Pope, July 17, 1734) continues the same moral concern: "And I make it my Last Request, that you continue that noble *Disdain* and *Abhorrence* of Vice, which you seem naturally endu'ed with, but still with a due regard to your own Safety; and study more to reform than chastise, tho' the one cannot be effected without the other."[27]

Death came on February 27, 1735, in his Cork Street home, and he was buried beside his wife in the Church of St. James's in Piccadilly on March 4. Swift, like many others, was heartbroken and wrote to Pope on May 12, "The Death of Mr Gay & the Doctor hath been terrible wounds near my heart. Their living would have been a great comfort to me, although I should never have seen them, like a Sum of Money in a Bank from which I should receive at least annual Interest. . . ."[28]

The death of Arbuthnot was indicative of the decline of the great Augustans. Addison had died in 1719, Steele and Congreve in 1729, Defoe in 1731, Gay in 1732. Pope and Swift were in their last decade, the Dean slipping into senility and the care of guardians and dying in 1745, and Pope's "long disease, my life" ending in 1744. The great neoclassical writers were dead or dying, their major works—*Gulliver's Travels, The Dunciad, The Beggar's Opera*, and others—already staples of the literary tradition, as a new generation—James Thomson, James Boswell, David Garrick, and Samuel Johnson—was rising to maturity and prominence. The great age of English satire, to which Arbuthnot had contributed so much, was almost at an end.

II A *"Man of Virtue and Sense"*

Bolingbroke, as we have seen, addressed Arbuthnot as a "man of virtue and sense," a judgment which few (except Dr. Woodward and John Flamsteed) of his contemporaries would have challenged. If the testimonies of a wide range of personalities can be trusted, the good doctor was a gentle and faithful friend, an able and sympathetic physician, and a pleasant companion, one of the most affable and convivial figures in an age notorious for its often intensely bitter literary rivalries. Although Arbuthnot had his enemies, none of his personal antipathies reached the intensity of those held by Addison, Defoe, Pope, Steele, and Swift.

Throughout his life in London, Arbuthnot showed a facility for making strong and enduring friendships among men of widely diverse personalities, talents, and attitudes. At Oxford, as early as 1694, he became a lifelong friend of Dr. Arthur Charlett, master of University College, and Dr. David Gregory, the eminent astronomer; Arbuthnot continued to correspond with Charlett as late as September 1712.[29] By 1698 he was acquainted with Thomas Creech, the translator of Horace and Lucretius, and had dined with the worldly Samuel Pepys, as yet unknown for his diary, who was to die five years later.[30]

The most fruitful years for gaining friendships came after 1711, for in this year, as we have seen, he probably met Swift and shortly thereafter Pope and Gay. His work as court physician, which had begun in 1709, brought him into close contact with Harley and Bolingbroke, the Duchess of Marlborough, and Queen Anne herself, to mention only the most notable. Steering as he did a quiet and moderate course through the turbulent seas of court politics and personalities, Arbuthnot moved with relative tranquility, apparently exciting little rancor or jealousy, dining and drinking with his literary friends, consulting with his colleagues about royal illnesses, but occasionally seeking a government favor for a relative, as when he sought an army captaincy for his brother George in 1711.[31] For the most part he seemed content to remain in the background and limit his political activities to the *John Bull* pamphlets, *The Art of Political Lying*, his correspondence, and his table-talk with his intimates, leaving more open and sustained partisanship to men like Swift. Upon leaving the court he spent the remainder of his life writing upon various topics, tending to his family, and ministering to his friends with his amiability and the limited medical arts of the early eighteenth century.

Of Arbuthnot's talents as a physician there is abundant evidence. At various times he attended not only the queen and her consort, Prince George, but also Swift, Pope, Congreve, the Duchess of Marlborough, Gay, William Pulteney, Martha Blount (the close friend of Pope), Lord Chesterfield, and Henrietta Howard (later Lady Suffolk). As Pope said in his letter of September 1, 1724, to Robert Digby, "I think him as good a Doctor as any man for one that is ill, and a better Doctor for one that is well."[32] As a practicing physician he was at work in an age when the great medical techniques were still far in the future, when some of the experiments fictionalized by Swift in Book III of *Gulliver's Travels* were not far removed from their originals as found in the *Philosophical Transactions* of the Royal Society, but letters of his friends attest to his skill. As late as 1775 Samuel Johnson felt that Arbuthnot was the exemplar of all that was good among medical men: "THERE are but two reasons for which a physician can decline the title of *Doctor of Medicine*, because he supposes himself disgraced by the doctorship, or supposes the doctorship disgraced by himself. To be disgraced by a title which he shares in common with every illustrious name of his profession, with Boerhave, with Arbuthnot, and with Cullen, can surely diminish no man's reputation."[33]

Arbuthnot had received his doctorate by examination at St. Andrews in 1696. Several days later, George Hamilton, principal at St. Andrews, wrote to Dr. Charlett, "The bearer, Dr. Arbuthnot, is a gentleman of great merit, that has acquitt himself extraordinarily well both in his private and publick tryalls in solemn meetings of several Professors and Doctors of Medicine towards his promotion."[34] In the following years Arbuthnot's effectiveness as a physician and sympathetic counselor is shown in his letters to Dr. Charlett regarding the misfortune of their mutual friend, Dr. Gregory, who, as he was dying of consumption, lost a child to smallpox (with which his other children were also afflicted).[35]

Perhaps representative of his medical work—and the state of early eighteenth-century medicine as well—is his advice in a letter of

December 11, 1718, to Swift, who was suffering one of his frequently recurring attacks of vertigo:

> glad at my heart I should be if Dr Helsham or I could do sow any good. . . . I have done good lately to a patient & a freind in that Complaint of a Vertigo by Cinnabar of Antimony & Castor, made up into Boluss with Confect of Alkermes. I had no great opinion of the Cinnabar, but trying it amongst other things, my freind found good of this prescription; I had tryd the Castor alone before; not with so much success. Small quantitys of Tinctur Sacr: now & then will do yow good.[36]

Crude and useless as these remedies seem today in the light of modern treatments of Ménière's Syndrome (labyrinthine vertigo), from which Swift suffered, they were as good as anything else offered by the pharmacopoeia of the early eighteenth century, but administered by a loving friend they may have offered some small psychosomatic relief.

The final estimates of contemporaries regarding Arbuthnot as a physician might very well be those of the philosopher George Berkeley, the worldly Lord Chesterfield, and Pope. Writing to Sir John Perceval on April 16, 1713, Berkeley says, "He is the Queen's domestic physician, and in great esteem with the whole Court, a great philosopher, and reckoned the first mathematician of the age, and has the character of uncommon virtue and probity."[37] Overly generous as this praise of Arbuthnot's mathematical and philosophical studies certainly is, it nevertheless is indicative of the esteem in which he was held by his friends.

Chesterfield was just as effusive and more extensive in his praise. Saying that Arbuthnot was both a physician and friend in whom he placed "utmost confidence," he feels that the doctor was professionally skillful and used his arts "with the most care and pleasure upon those unfortunate patients, who could not give him a fee." He was, furthermore, a man of "great and various erudition" who possessed "an infinite fund of wit and humour, to which his friends Pope and Swift were more obliged, than they have acknowledged themselves to be." His "almost inexhaustible" imagination seemed to be "at any body's service, for as soon as he was exonerated he did not care what became of it," sometimes allowing his young sons to make kites out of "his scattered papers of hints, which would have furnished good matter for folios." His lack of jealousy and possessiveness permitted others to borrow extensively from his ideas

to produce "a rich vein of ore"; and his indifference to his own
reputation as a writer prevented him from paying more attention to
the publication of his works. In short, says Chesterfield, the man
was marked by "charity, benevolence, and a love of mankind . . .
in all he said or did," a man who "lived and died a devout and
sincere Christian . . . who took leave of us with tenderness, without
weakness, and told us that he died, not only with the comfort, but
even the devout assurance, of a Christian."[38]
   But the most eloquent tribute is that of Pope at the end of his
famous *Epistle from Mr. Pope, to Dr. Arbuthnot* (written 1731 -
1734; published 1735):

> O Friend! may each Domestick Bliss be thine!
> Be no unpleasing Melancholy mine:
> Me, let the tender Office long engage
> To rock the Cradle of reposing Age,
> With lenient Arts extend a Mother's breath,
> Make Languour smile, and smooth the Bed of Death,
> Explore the Thought, explain the asking Eye,
> And keep a while one Parent from the Sky!
> On Cares like these if Length of days attend,
> May Heav'n, to bless those days, preserve my Friend,
> Preserve him social, chearful, and serene,
> And just as rich as when he serv'd a QUEEN!
> Whether that Blessing be deny'd or giv'n,
> Thus far was right, the rest belongs to Heav'n.[39]

   Like any other human being Arbuthnot also possessed some
endearing idiosyncrasies commented upon by his friends. Apparently, for example, there was an odd movement to his walk, as Pope
quotes Swift on September 1, 1724 ("He is a Man that can do
everything but walk"[40]), and as Swift himself writes to Pope about a
year later (September 29, 1725): "So our Doctor has every Quality
and Virtue that can make a man amiable or usefull, but alas he hath
a sort of Slouch in his walk."[41] And there was also his fascination
with card games, which drew the attention of Pope, Lord Chesterfield, Lady Hervey, and the *Gentleman's Magazine.* Pope reports to
Swift on September 3, 1726, that "The Dr. goes to cards, Gay to
Court; one loses money, one loses his time."[42] Five years later
Chesterfield tells Arbuthnot that Lady Murray "told me . . . that
you had been melancholy, ever since you had been most shamefully
beaten at cards by the superior good play of a French Spaniel lately

brought over,"[43] a teasing remark based perhaps on a report in the *Gentleman's Magazine* of February 1731: "The famous French bitch, that plays at cards, and performs many wonderful tricks, beat Dr. Arbuthnot 2 games at quadrille."[44] And, also in 1731 (June 19), Lady Hervey writes to the Countess of Suffolk: "I hear that Dr. Arbuthnot is gone to Tunbridge: I wish he may not fill his belly more than his pocket; I am sure he will do so if John Dories and quadrille players are plenty this season."[45]

Arbuthnot took these and other pleasantries with grace, for they were marks of endearment for an eminent medical man, a gentle and decent doctor who exemplified the finest aspects of the age: a lively intellectual curiosity which ranged into various scientific areas; a witty mind which produced several memorable satires; and a personality congenial to the greatest talents of his day—Harley and Bolingbroke in politics; Newton and Wren and Halley in science; and, among the literary men, Pope, Swift, Addison, Gay, Chesterfield, and Congreve, to name the most famous. Every period has such a man as Dr. Arbuthnot, but all too often he becomes lost in the brilliant aura of the more notorious, the self-seeking, the tendentious. The quiet career of Dr. Arbuthnot, moving easily through the court, tending to the medical needs of the great, the near-great, and the charity cases, playing cards, taking an interest in music and the other arts, and enjoying his family, is as much a part of the age of Queen Anne as the more famous doings of his friends. He indeed was the "perfectly honest man" and a "man of virtue and sense."

CHAPTER 2

Minor Political Works

A LTHOUGH Arbuthnot lived in politically tempestuous times
and moved in a circle of men who were active in political
affairs, he himself remained relatively aloof from the extremes of
controversy and the day-to-day maneuvering at court and in Parliament. Close as he was to Swift, Gay, and the other Tory wits, he
rarely seems to have permitted their political animosities and causes
to become his own. Characterized by Lord Chesterfield as "a
Jacobite by prejudice, and a Republican by reflection and
reasoning," Arbuthnot tended to be chary of overt political involvement, especially in print. Probably somewhat constrained by his
position in the royal household and his own aversion to publicity
and strident partisanship, he chose to remain the perceptive and
amused observer whose thoughts on politics were embodied public-
ly only in several light satires and a sermon.

Whereas Swift wrote voluminously (and rarely with any degree of
objectivity) on the complex problems of church-state relationships,
English domestic and foreign policy, and the Treaty of Utrecht, and
while Gay could flay Prime Minister Robert Walpole in *The
Beggar's Opera*, Arbuthnot commented only occasionally on
political matters in his correspondence. Only *The History of John
Bull* (to be discussed in Chapter 3) and *The Art of Political Lying*
deal with the political traumas of Queen Anne's reign at any length,
while another piece—*A Sermon Preach'd to the People at the
Mercat-Cross of Edinburgh* (1706)—discusses rather soberly the advantages of the proposed union of England and Scotland which was
to be consummated the following year. Four other minor works are
also political in nature, and will be discussed later in this chapter:
The Humble Petition of the Colliers (1716), *The Quidnuncki's: A
Tale* and *Reasons Humbly Offered by the Upholders* (both 1724),
and *An Epitaph on Francis Charteris* (1732). The last is the only
work of Arbuthnot's which descends into a harsh and personal satire
upon an individual.

32

I   *A Sermon. . . at the Mercat-Cross*

The political relationship between England and Scotland had been especially strained since the deposition of James II, a Stuart and a Scotsman, and the coronation of William II and James's daughter Mary in 1689, by which William became King of England but not of Scotland.[1] A majority of the Scots accepted William as head of state, but a minority still held a strong loyalty to James, a nationalistic and emotional connection which would cause difficulties for the English in the rebellions of 1715 and 1745. Consequently, William found his political and religious control of Scotland at best uneasy, and more than occasionally he had to resort to military force to assert his authority and right. And in order to create stability in Scotland after the brutal massacre of the Scots at Glencoe (1692), he was forced to restore Presbyterianism as the established church in Scotland and grant the Scottish Parliament greater political independence than it had hitherto known. But these conciliatory changes did not seem to settle the issues or silence the voices of Scots nationalism, and thus William felt it necessary to work toward a union of England and Scotland, but he died in 1702 before his proposal had been carried very far.

The continuing antagonism—the Scots wanting a monarchial succession divorced from that of England, and the English Parliament legislating increasingly narrower restrictions on Scottish trade—influenced both nations to negotiate terms for the union, which was to be completed in the Act of Union (1707), providing for Scottish representation in the English Parliament, an adjudication of outstanding financial obligations to the benefit of Scotland, the removal of trade restrictions, and the preservation of Scottish legal, political, and religious institutions on the local level. This agreement should have pleased everyone but the extremists.

The proposed union, however, was unpopular among many north of the Tweed and remained so for several decades after its achievement (and the renewed Scottish national movement in recent years suggests that its spirit still is). Arbuthnot, though a Scot to the bone, saw the advantages of union for Scotland and ably argued them in the *Sermon*. The preface, probably written by William Duncombe for the 1745 edition, summarizes the twenty-three articles and the inherent advantages.

But it is in the sermon proper that Arbuthnot's own desire for political stability and the well-being of Scotland is seen. Using as his scriptural text a passage from the apocryphal *Ecclesiasticus*

(10:27)—"Better is he that laboureth, and aboundeth in all things, than he that boasteth himself and wanteth bread"—he begins by asking his audience to bridle their passions for a time in order to listen to his appeal and telling them that

a generous, a powerful, a victorious nation invites you to an intimate union with themselves, a nation whose laws are more just, whose government is more mild, whose people are more free, easy, and happy, than any other in Europe; a nation who by their wealth, wisdom, and valour, have broke the most formidable power that ever threatened Christendom; to whose victorious arms even you yourselves owe your present security.[2]

He gently chides the Scots for having received the proposal for union with "riots, mobs, and tumults," and suggests that they suspend their prejudices in order to give the matter a full hearing, something as difficult then as it is now on issues affecting a people's economic, political, or religious interests.

Appealing to common sense and self-interest, Arbuthnot demonstrates that the only alternative to this union is a traumatic one of a different sort, with "three dismal companions, pride, poverty, and idleness" (p. 397); after all, "it is better to increase our trade, manufacture, and riches by union with England, than to boast of our sovereignty, and starve" (pp. 397 - 98). He then moves on to argue that if the union is brought about, all Scotland will benefit through new trade opportunities, increased employment, improved living conditions, and greater political power. Refusal of these advantages, Arbuthnot tells the Scots, would be "a witness against your matchless ignorance and stupidity" (p. 402).

In the second part Arbuthnot strikes down the argument that Scotland will lose her sovereignty and identity by the union. Admitting that Scotland will always be less powerful in her influence upon British affairs than will England, he shows that Scottish independence under the current scheme of things is a chimera and that the union will be a better safeguard of Scotland's interests (pp. 404 - 405).

In his conclusion Arbuthnot charges that opponents to the union are either opportunists using the issue for their own questionable benefit or "persons of honour, who have as true a sense of liberty, and as great a concern for the welfare of their country as any." If only the former will lay aside their "unreasonable humour" and the latter their prejudices, "their judgments will quickly inform them of the proposal." Obviously, to Arbuthnot, to govern a free people, is a far more noble and honourable character, than to insult over slaves and beggars; and if any such there be, who hug their chains, and are fond of their rags, and, as wretched people once did by the Romans, refuse their liberty when offered, they are unworthy so generous and beneficial a proposal. (p. 408)

Arbuthnot ends by offering the Scots a resplendent vision of all that will be theirs if they accept and support the union:

Consider, then, in this your day, the happy conditions of your neighbouring nation: survey their verdant fields, their beautiful plantations and sumptuous gardens, where culture, art, and expenses reign; their populous and flourishing cities. View the magnificence of their public structures; the neatness, cleanliness, conveniency, and costly furniture of their private houses: consider the liberty and plenty of their meanest commoners; the comfortable estates which even the lowest of their tradesmen leave to their families; the immense riches of their merchants; the grandeur and magnificence of the learned societies; and the prodigious stocks of their trading companies; the unconquerable force of their fleets and armies; the justice and exact execution of their laws; and the wise administration of their government: ponder all these things, and then sure you will not reckon them your enemies, who offer you a partnership in so great blessings; but will conclude with the wise man in my text: "Better is he that laboureth, and aboundeth in all things, than he that boasteth himself and wanteth bread. (p. 408)

There is no way by which we can judge the effect of Arbuthnot's sermon upon Scottish attitudes toward the union, but its influence may have been negligible. Lost amid the flood of similar pamphlets and speeches on the subject, it perhaps had as little impact upon feelings rooted in tradition and nationalistic self-interest as does its counterpart in any other time and place. Instead, the value of the sermon lies in its reflection of the issues which irritated English-Scottish relationships in the period after 1660 and in its demonstration of the author's characteristic good sense and moderation. The argumentation is orderly, pointed, and fluent, devoid of passion, persuasive. Arbuthnot, though advocating a course unpopular among many of his countrymen, fulfills a higher kind of Scottish patriotism which views union as the best and most practical means of assuring the continued greatness and security of Scotland and of building a solid, prosperous, and peaceful nation. But despite the even temper of this sermon, Arbuthnot could, as we shall see in the next chapter, treat the Scots satirically.

II   The Art of Political Lying

The year 1712 saw the publication of a series of political satires consisting of the *John Bull* pamphlets and the much shorter *Art of Political Lying*, all of which had their source in the Tory-Whig agitation of the last years of the reign of Queen Anne.

At a time when political rancor was at its height and when the nation was badly torn over the issues of ending or continuing the ten-year-old War of the Spanish Succession, which the Tory ministry of Robert Harley (Oxford) and Henry St. John (Bolingbroke) had been trying to end in the face of strong opposition by the Whigs, Arbuthnot published *The Art of Political Lying* in October. Amusing as it certainly is, this little satire does not suggest the tenor of the intense and bitter political quarrels or the intricate diplomatic negotiations; for a better view of such complex matters one might instead turn to works written by Swift during these same years: the famous *Journal to Stella* (letters to Esther Johnson, September 1, 1710, to June 6, 1713), *The Conduct of the Allies* (1711), *The History of the Four Last Years of the Queen* (1713), and *An Enquiry into the Behavior of the Queen's Last Ministry* (printed posthumously, 1765). Swift had descended into the cockpit of political debate and chicanery, wounding and being wounded, but Arbuthnot, sympathetic as he was to the troubles of Swift and the Tories, contented himself with a more distant view of a recurrent problem: the use of language for propaganda and polemic.

The idea of a satire on political manipulation of truth was certainly not unique in the early eighteenth century with Arbuthnot, for the topic attracted the talents of Swift (*Examiner*, Numbers 14 and 15 for November 9 and 16, 1710), Addison (*Spectator*, Number 305 for February 19, 1712), and the anonymous author of Numbers VI, VIII, XIII, and XIV of the Tory *Plain Dealer* for May 17 and 31, July 5 and 12, 1712. Arbuthnot was probably familiar with all of these, certainly those of Swift and Addison, but just how far they influenced his own work cannot be determined. All, except for Addison's *Spectator* piece, were directed against the Whigs, but Arbuthnot, except for a couple of anti-Whig references, is far more detached in his satire upon the opposition to Harley and Bolingbroke. Swift thought it good enough to recommend to Esther Johnson, writing her on October 9, 1712, that "Arbuthnot has sent me from Windsor a pretty Discourse upon Lying, and I have ordered the Printer to come for it. . . . Pray get it when it comes out,"[3] and two months later (December 12) that "The Pamphlet of

Politicall Lying is writt by Dr Arbuthnot the Authr of John Bull, tis very pretty; but not so obvious to be understood."[4]

Arbuthnot's little satire—its full title is *Proposals for Printing a very Curious Discourse, in Two Volumes in Quarto, entitled* ΨΕΥΔΟΑΦΙΑ ΤΟΑΙΤΚΗ, *or, A Treatise of the Art of Political Lying*—is in two parts. The first is an announcement of the proposed printing of the first volume at Hilary Term (January 13), the price and terms of subscription, and the places where subscriptions may be entered. The second is an abstract of the eleven chapters of the first volume.

The first volume, according to the prospectus, will deal with the nature of the soul and its propensity for lying: "the tendency of the soul towards the malicious springs from self-love, or a pleasure to find mankind more wicked, base, or unfortunate than ourselves." The second chapter defines political lying as "the art of convincing the people of salutary falsehoods, for some good end" (p. 295) and shows that this species of falsehood has been invaluable to English politicians before and after the revolution of 1688 and that it can be used most effectively by three kinds of men: "One man spreads a lie to sell and buy stock to a greater advantage; a second, because it is honourable to serve his party; and a third, because it is sweet to gratify his revenge" (p. 295).

In the abstract of the third chapter the author tries to prove the moral rightness of political lying. He admits that the people have a right to truth in family, financial, and other private matters, "but that they have no right at all to Political Truth" (pp. 295 - 96), and in the fourth, posing as "a true friend to English liberty," determines that political prevarication is a right of the people;

that, as the government of England has a mixture of democratical in it, so the right of inventing and spreading Political Lies is partly in the people; and their obstinate adherence to this just privilege has been most conspicuous, and shined with great lustre of late years: that it happens very often, that there are no means left to the good people of England to pull down a ministry and government they are weary of, but by exercising this their undoubted right: that abundance of Political Lying is a sure sign of true English liberty: that, as ministers do sometimes use tools to support their power, it is but reasonable that people should employ the same weapon to defend themselves and pull them down. (p. 296)

The proposed fifth chapter divides political lies into several types: the "additory" inflates a man's reputation so that he may serve a good purpose; the "detractory" takes from him his just reputation so as to prevent his harming the public; and the "translatory" transfers a man's good or bad actions to another (pp. 296 - 98). The sixth chapter shows that the "miraculous" lie, subdivided into "terrifying" and "animating or encouraging" lies, may be used to excellent advantage, and gives rules for the proper application of these techniques (pp. 297 - 98).

The seventh chapter takes up the question as to which party—Tory or Whig—is most adept at lying, and it is here that Arbuthnot drops his mask for a moment to let his own Tory sympathies emerge: "The Tories have been better believed of late, but . . . the Whigs have much the greater geniuses among them,"[5] though both factions have glutted the market with falsehood. The situation, however, is not without a remedy by which the Whigs may restore their credibility as liars: "the party should agree to vent nothing but truth for three months together, which will give them credit for six months' lying afterwards."[6] Ironically, the persona-editor calls the scheme "chimerical," since even the author "believes it almost impossible to find fit persons to execute this scheme"; no politician is capable of telling the truth, and the parties dare not rely upon newswriters, even to tell lies (pp. 299 - 300).

Arbuthnot's distrust of the Whigs appears again in the eighth chapter as the author proposes combining smaller groups of liars into a single society, made up of all the professions, to whom will be committed the responsibility for supervision of all lying. This society will make it a crime "for anybody to talk of anything but the lie of the day" and will take steps to place spies at court, furnish hints for lies, expel any of its members embarrassed by their falsehoods, and "establish a private committee for whispers" (p. 301). Arbuthnot then again digresses to give the back of his hand to the Whigs; as the mock-editor tells us,

Here the author makes a digression in praise of the Whig party, for the right understanding and use of proof-lies. A proof-lie is like a proof-charge for a piece of ordnance, to try a standard credulity. Of such a nature he takes transubstantiation to be in the Church of Rome, a proof-article, which if any one swallows, they are sure he will digest everything else: therefore the Whig party do wisely to try the credulity of the people sometimes by swingers, that they may be able to judge to what height they may charge them afterwards. (p. 301)

The author warns, however, that these politicians must not make the mistake of believing their own lies, which has proved of pernicious consequence of late, both a wise party and a wise nation having regulated their affairs upon lies of their own invention. The causes of this he supposes to be too great a zeal and intenseness in the practice of this art, and a vehement heat in mutual conversation, whereby they persuade one another that what they wish, and report to be true, is really so: that all parties have been subject to this misfortune. The Jacobites have been constantly infested with it; but the Whigs of late seemed even to exceed them in this ill habit and weakness. (p. 301)

The ninth and tenth chapters deal with the "celerity," speed of travel, and "characteristics of lies; how to know when, where, and by whom invented," and "whether a lie is best contradicted by truth, or by another lie," the answer to the latter in the eleventh and final chapter being that "the properest contradiction to a lie is another lie":

For example, if it should be reported, that the Pretender was at London, one would not contradict it by saying he was never in England; but you must prove by eye-witnesses that he came no farther than Greenwich, and then went back again. (p. 302)

The essay ends abruptly with the promise (never fulfilled and probably not intended to be) that the abstract of "the second volume of this excellent treatise is reserved for another time" (p. 303).

Thus Arbuthnot satirizes the tampering with truth so common and tempting to politicians and journalists in all times and places. His satire in this piece is mild, gentle, Horatian in manner, so different from the more acerb political commentary of Pope, Swift, and Gay. A personality more combative and hungry for political power or preferment might have been strongly tempted to employ the backstairs gossip of the court and the parliamentary benches, as well as the public and private idiosyncrasies of leading politicians, to make his satire more slashing. Arbuthnot does not allude to specific issues, nor does he provide any thinly veiled portraits of the exemplars of the political liar; he is satisfied to generalize, to avoid the name-calling so rampant in political quarrels, whether in the eighteenth century or the twentieth. But as we shall see in the next chapter, Arbuthnot could occasionally make his satire more personal and specific, as he did in the *John Bull* pamphlets and in his attack upon a notorious rake. In spirit *The Art of Political Lying* is closer to the *Spectator* and the *Tatler* of Addison and Steele than to the more strident and subjective satire of Swift. The modern reader will have no trouble in applying the lessons of Arbuthnot's little piece to a world in which politicians often operate by news leaks, press releases, and pretensions to public interest, and in which journalists sometimes mask theft and character assassination under the ideal of the people's right to know the truth.

III   The Humble Petition

Aside from *The Art of Political Lying* and *The History of John Bull*, Arbuthnot wrote only four other pieces of political satire, all of them brief. Like much of his other satire, they are for the most part Horatian in tone, and only the epitaph on Francis Charteris, one of the most notorious eighteenth-century rakes, partakes of the kind of bitterness which permeates Swift's ironic elegy on the Duke of Marlborough or Pope's vicious attack on John, Lord Hervey in the "Sporus" section of his verse epistle to Arbuthnot.

The first of these is a pamphlet which bears the full title *To the Right Honourable The Mayor and Aldermen of the City of London. The Humble Petition of the Colliers, Cooks, Cook-Maids, Blacksmiths, Jackmakers, Braziers and Others*. It appeared as a single folio sheet in 1716 and reappeared in 1732 as part of the third volume of the *Miscellanies* printed by Benjamin Motte and again in Volume III of Charles Bathurst's *Miscellanies* (1742). A *jeu d'esprit*, it affects to be a protest against a group of "virtuosi disaffected to the government and to the trade and prosperity of this kingdom," who call themselves the "CATOPTRICAL VICTUALLERS"[7] and purport to be able to use mirrors (catoptrics) and sunbeams for culinary purposes. These experimenters, reminiscent of the assorted scientific madmen and medical quacks who run amok through so much of the satiric literature of the Restoration and eighteenth century,

have presumed by gathering, breaking, folding, and bundling up the sunbeams by the help of certain glasses, to make, produce, and kindle up several new focuses or fires within these his Majesty's dominions, and thereby to boil, bake, stew, fry, and dress all sorts of victuals and provisions, to brew, distil spirits, smelt ore, and in general to perform all the offices of ordinary fires, and are endeavouring to procure to themselves the monopoly of this their said invention. (p. 375)

The petitioners proceed to demonstrate that the continuation of these new methods of using fire will "utterly ruin and reduce to beggary" themselves, their families and servants, and the trades which depend upon them; they will have no other work left them "but warming of cellars and dressing of suppers in the winter time." The new arts of fire will also ruin navigation and the tallow-chandlers, upon whose product the government levies a tax, thus seriously impairing an important source of the politicians' revenue (pp. 375 - 76).

Not only this, but the virtuosi also profane the sun's rays by using them to roast oxen on the Thames River in winter, thus encroaching upon the rights of the watermen. The public will also be greatly discomfited since the sun shines at different times in various parts of the city; this "will occasion great irregularity as to the time of dining of the several inhabitants, and consequently great uncertainty and confusion in the despatch of business: and to those, who by reason of their northern exposition will still be forced to be at the expense of culinary fires, it will reduce the price of their manufacture to such inequality, as is inconsistent with common justice: and the same inconveniency will affect the landlords in the values of their rents" (p. 376).

Furthermore, a good many of the petitioners will have to study optics and astronomy in order to use these new methods, a task many of them are incapable of mastering. The new technology "will throw the whole art of cookery into the hands of astronomers and glass-grinders, persons utterly unskilled in other parts of that profession, to the great detriment of health of his Majesty's good subjects" (p. 376).

The petitioners strengthen their case by citing evidence (drawn from what they call experience) that meat cooked by the new methods is unhealthy, several partakers already having died, for "the sunbeams taken inwardly render the humours too hot and adust, occasion great sweatings, and dry up the radical moisture" (pp. 376 - 77). The sunbeams also adversely affect the brain, causing "madness and distraction at the time of the full moon." And this "inward light" will also spread Quakerism to endanger the Church and encourage Popery to the peril of the government. Furthermore, the sunbeams will also enter the blood, and when the sun is in the signs of Aries, Taurus, and Capricorn ("the horned signs"), there will appear "such a spirit of unchastity as is dangerous to the honour of your worships' families" (p. 377).

Finally, since mankind feeds much upon seeds and plants, there is a further danger that the sunbeams in the body may cause these seeds to germinate in the stomach, particularly among the poor,

who are most confined to a vegetable diet. And if a long eclipse
should strike the city, its inhabitants, denied the customary methods
of cooking, will be hard-pressed for subsistence and survival
(p. 377). The satire ends with the "humble petition":

Therefore, the petitioners, in light of this evidence . . . humbly pray that
your honours would either totally prohibit the confining and manufacturing
the sunbeams for any of the useful arts of life, or in the ensuing parliament
procure a tax to be laid upon them, which may answer both the price and
duty of coals, and which we humbly conceive cannot be less than thirty
shillings per yard square, reserving the sole right and privilege of the catoptrical cookery to the Royal Society, and to the commanders and crew of the
bomb-vessel, under the direction of Mr. Whiston for finding out the
longitude, who by reason of the remoteness of their stations, may be reduced to straits for want of firing.
     And we likewise beg that your honours, as to the forementioned points,
would hear the Reverend Flamsteed, who is the legal officer appointed by
the government to look after the heavenly luminaries, whom we have con-
stituted our trusty and learned solicitor. (pp. 377 - 78)

     Thus Arbuthnot provides an amusing satire upon both the ex-
periments of the virtuosi (and his colleagues of the Royal Society,
perhaps) and the layman's fear of new developments in science, as
well as a parody of technical writing. By means of hyperbole,
specious logic, and time-honored warnings about the safety of
Church and State, Arbuthnot mocks both the universal tendency of
people to view the new and threateningly unfamiliar with alarm,
and the scientific projectors who develop their theories with
arrogance and disregard for the welfare of the public. The scientists
seem to be as crackbrained as their counterparts in Book III of
Swift's *Gulliver's Travels*, and the satire is all the more delightful
because of Arbuthnot's expertise. In passing he does not hesitate to
take a slap at his old enemy John Flamsteed, with whom he had
been involved in the controversy over the star-catalogues less than a
decade before; and he also alludes to the efforts of William Whiston
to demonstrate a method of determining longitude in his book
(written with Humphrey Ditton) *A New Method of Discovering the
Longitude* (1714). The petitioners, with their economic and political
fears, are, however, no less foolish than the experimenters who, with
Sir Francis Bacon, have taken all knowledge to be their province.

IV   Reasons Humbly Offered by the . . . Upholders

Another satire of the same sort is *Reasons Humbly Offered By the Company Exercising the Trade and Mystery of Upholders, Against Part of the Bill for the Better Viewing, Searching, and Examining Drugs, Medicines, &c, 1724.* This satire had its origin in the old controversy (see, for example, Dr. Samuel Garth's mock-epic, *The Dispensary*, 1699) between the physicians and apothecaries over the right to prescribe drugs. The College of Physicians had sought to prevent the apothecaries from dispensing drugs without a doctor's prescription; an act later passed Parliament giving the Censors of the College a right to visit the shops of the apothecaries to examine their stocks. Arbuthnot's satire was only one of a large number of tracts which appeared during the controversy.

The upholders—that is, the undertakers—protest the proposed bill with the encouragement of the apothecaries, "in regard of our common interest, and in gratitude to the said retailers and dispensers of medicines, which we have always found to be very effectual . . ." (p. 379). The act under debate in Parliament, say the morticians, will hinder trade and, in particular, woolen manufacture (a parliamentary act of almost a half century before required corpses to be wrapped in wool before burial). The upholders, who generally have had no complaints from their clientele, claim that the law "is a manifest encroachment on the liberty and property of the subject," for it will unreasonably delay the people's enjoyment of their right to death and burial. Furthermore, the present mode of medical prescription is absolutely necessary to the stability of English society:

We hope that it will be considered, that there are multitudes of necessitous heirs and penurious parents, persons in pinching circumstances with numerous families of children, wives that have lived long, many robust aged women with great jointures, elder brothers with bad understandings, single heirs of great estates, whereby the collateral lines are forever excluded, reversionary patents, and reversionary promises of preferments, leases upon single lives, and play-debts upon joint lives, and that the persons so aggrieved have no hope of being speedily relieved any other way than by the dispensing of drugs and medicines in the manner they now are; burying alive being judged repugnant to the known laws of this kingdom. (p. 380)

Furthermore, there are a good many living dead who, but for the intervention of the government, would have been in the hands of the morticians. Frequent funerals serve to provide genealogies and bring honors, support the needy clergy and clerks and mourners, and give employment to the old coaches of the nobility. Finally, "we further hope that frequent funerals will not be discouraged, as is by this bill proposed, it being the only method left of carrying some people to church" (pp. 380 - 81).

Therefore, Parliament must not "introduce an arbitrary and unlimited power for people to live (in defiance of art) as long as they can by the course of nature, to the prejudice of our Company, and the decay of trade" (p. 381). And as a final thought, the undertakers plead that coffin-making be reserved to the manufacturers of caskets and that

the interests of the several trades and professions which depend upon ours may be regarded; such as that of hearses, coaches, coffins, epitaphs, and bell-ropes, stone-cutters, feather-men, and bell-ringers; and especialy the manufacturers of crapes, and the makers of snuff, who use great quantities of old coffins, and who, considered in the consumption of their drugs, employ by far the greatest number of hands of any manufacture of the kingdom. (p. 381)

As a physician Arbuthnot probably felt very strongly about the integrity of medicine, for then, as now, the profession was under attack from various quarters. In satirizing the undertakers and apothecaries he attacks those who make money from the miseries of others, the economic and social parasites who feed upon the fears and agonies of humanity. It is ironic that at almost the same time of the publication of this satire, Swift was at work on Book IV of *Gulliver's Travels*, where physicians are bitterly savaged by Gulliver as he tells the Master Houyhnhnm of the English doctors and concludes with a charge against them similar to that made by Arbuthnot against the apothecaries: "They are likewise of special Use to Husbands and Wives, who are grown weary of their Mates; to eldest Sons, to great Ministers of State, and often to Princes."[8] Arbuthnot's private reaction to Swift's satire in this instance was probably mixed as he admired the wit and squirmed at the satire against his own profession.

V   The Quidnuncki's

Another political satire appeared in 1724: *A Poem Address'd to the Quidnunc's, at St. James's Coffee House London. Occasion'd by the Death of the Duke of Orleans*, later titled *The Quidnuncki's* when republished in 1727. The work is a satire on political rumor and newsmongers, a kind of satire found elsewhere in the period, as for example in five of Richard Steele's *Tatlers* (Numbers 10, 155, 160, 178, and 232 for May 3, 1709, and April 6 and 18, May 30, and October 3, 1710), Joseph Addison's *Spectator* Number 625 (November 26, 1714), and Pope's *Dunciad*.[9] Though this poem of forty-eight lines in octosyllabic couplets has been attributed to Gay, Pope, or Swift, it is undoubtedly Arbuthnot's.[10]

The form of the poem is a short dramatic dialogue between a "Master Travers," who is upset by news of the death of Philippe, the Duke of Orleans and Regent of France, as well as by his own fears of the possible consequences for England at the hands of the Czar, the Turks, and the Pope, and an India-merchant, who ridicules these apprehensions by telling him of a race of monkeys by the Ganges River:

> Grave, Sober, Sage, like you Quidnunc[i]'s,
> On either Bank, from Bough to Bough,
> They meet and chat, as we do now.
> Whispers go round: They grin, they shrug;
> They bow, they smile, they scratch, they hug;
> And, just as Chance or Whim provoke'em,
> They either bite their Friends, or Stroak'em.[11]

Among them is an "active Prig" who likes to show his gymnastic superiority over his fellows while "the chattering Tribe admire." He swings from side to side "And bangs his Foes and Friends by Turns," but

> Crack goes the Twig, and in he flounces,
> Down the swift Stream the Wretch is born,
> Never, ah never to return!
> Hah what a Fall has our dear Brother!
> Morbleau, cries one, Hela, says t'other.
> The Nations give a general Screech;
> None cocks his *Tail;* none claws his *Breech.*
> Each trembles for the publick Weal,
> And for a while forgets to steal.[12]

They watch him swirl out of sight, but he is replaced by another aspirant on the highest branch, and the show begins again: "*And business on each Monkey Shore,/Runs the same Track it ran before.*"[13]

Thus Arbuthnot satirizes the continuing human fascination with political speculation, rumor, and needless fears of inconsequential events. Having lived for a long time amid the intrigues of the court, having seen statesmen and politicians come and go, and having watched the ebb and flow of gossip and rumor, he is undisturbed by changes in faces on the political scene; no matter what happens, the world will continue on its course. Thus the Quidnunc ("What now?"—as in the case of the letter-writer Thomas Quid-nunc in Addison's *Spectator* Number 625)[14] wastes his time worrying about what is often trivia. Arbuthnot might well agree with Steele's comment in *Tatler* Number 178: "What I am now warning the people of is, that the newspapers of this island are as pernicious to weak heads in England as ever books of chivalry to Spain; and therefore shall do all that in me lies, with the utmost care and vigilance imaginable, to prevent these growing evils."[15]

Arbuthnot's handling of the beast fable is competent and his use of the Hudibrastic verse is effective enough, but somehow the poem lacks the force and humor of the character of the political upholsterer in *Tatlers* 155, 160, 178, and 232, that ubiquitous retailer of rumor who neglects his business and his family while talking with, and sending letters to, Isaac Bickerstaff.[16] The poem is just another example of Arbuthnot's concern with those human characteristics which in moderation are good but become subjects for satire in their excess.

VI   "An Epitaph on Francis Charteris"

As we have seen in the satires discussed in this chapter, and as will be shown in the major works to be considered in the next chapter, Arbuthnot's satire is rarely personal or savage, something which cannot be said so easily for the work of many of his contemporaries. But the last of his minor satires departs from the gentler tones of the earlier works to provide a vicious attack upon Francis Charteris (or Chartres), one of the most notorious rakes of the early eighteenth century. Published anonymously in April 1732 in both the *London Magazine* and the *Gentleman's Magazine*, "An Epitaph on Francis Charteris" attacks the man for all kinds of public and private depravity.

Charteris was well known to his contemporaries, and Arbuthnot was not the only Augustan to comment upon the man's debauchery and crimes. Pope, in a note to his own "Epistle III: To Allen Lord Bathurst" (1733, dated 1732), describes him thus:

FR. CHARTRES, a man infamous for all manner of vices. When he was an ensign in the army he was drumm'd out of the regiment for a cheat; he was next banish'd at Brussels, and drumm'd out of Ghent on the same account. After a hundred tricks at the gaming-tables, he took to lending of money at exorbitant interests and on great penalties, accumulating premium, and capital into a new capital, and seizing to a minute when the payment became due; in a word, by a constant attention to the vices, wants, and follies of mankind, he acquired an immense fortune. His house was a perpetual bawdy-house. He was twice condemn'd for rapes, and pardoned: but the last time not without imprisonment in Newgate, and large confiscations. He died in Scotland in 1731, aged 62. The populace at his funeral rais'd a great riot, almost tore the body out of the coffin, and cast dead dogs, &c. into the grave along with it. . . . This Gentleman was *worth seven thousand pounds a year* estate in Land, and about one hundred *thousand in Money.*[17]

Swift, too, pilloried Charteris in lines 49 - 54 of his "An Excellent New Ballad: or, The True En - - - sh D - - n to be Hang'd for a Rape" (1730), an attack upon Dr. Thomas Sawbridge, Dean of Ferns, indicted for rape but acquitted, and in lines 189 - 90 of his "Verses on the Death of Dr. Swift" (1731).[18] If these were not enough to preserve the infamy of Charteris, his story was told to later eighteenth-century readers in *The Newgate Calendar* (1771), a collection of crime stories,[19] and he is thought to be pictured in the first plate of William Hogarth's series of paintings *The Harlot's Progress* (1732).[20]

Arbuthnot characterizes Charteris as a man who tirelessly and constantly, despite his age and failing strength, practiced every vice known to man except hypocrisy and prodigality. Avaricious, impudent, and depraved,

> He was the only person of his time
> Who could cheat without the mask of honesty,
> Retain his primeval meanness when possessed of
>   Ten Thousand a year:
> Was at last condemned to it for what he could not do.
>   Oh indignant reader!
> Think not his life useless to mankind;
> Providence connived at his execrable designs,
> To give after-ages a conspicuous
> Proof and example
> Of how small estimation is exorbitant wealth
> In the sight of God, by his bestowing it on
> The most unworthy of all mortals.[21]

Arbuthnot would have been grimly amused to read in *The Newgate Calendar* of Charteris's conviction at Old Bailey with tied thumbs and the inscription below his picture:

> Blood!—must a colonel, with a lord's estate,
> Be thus obnoxious to a scoundrel's fate?
> Brought to the bar, and sentenc'd from the bench,
> Only for ravishing a country wench?[22]

Arbuthnot's attack on Charteris does not rise above the level of lampoon, nor does it come close to achieving the bitterness or intensity of Swift's savagery toward the Duke of Marlborough in his "Satirical Elegy on the Death of a Late Famous General" (1722) or of Robert Browning's "To Edward Fitzgerald" (1889), but it does show that the usually amiable and charitable physician could write as wrathfully as his friends frequently did.

VII   *"More to Reform than to Chastise"*

The shorter and occasional pieces examined in this chapter, published from 1706 to 1732 and spanning the whole period of Arbuthnot's public career, reflect the personality of an intelligent and sensitive man of firm principle who viewed the failings of his society with gentleness and tolerance (though occasionally, as in the epitaph on Charteris, descending to the personal lampoon). Although there is never any doubt as to his moral stance, the tone of his satire is most often like that of Fielding and Gay and only rarely similar to that of Pope and Swift. He is content to observe human nature and its failings, to chide in a gently Horatian manner, and then to let the world go on its way. The politicians, journalists, and extremists of *The Act of Political Lying*, the stubborn Scots addressed in the *Sermon . . . at the Mercat Cross*, the fearful petitioners among the upholders and the fireworkers, and the decadent Charteris—all are part of the human comedy that Arbuthnot knew, and on each he played his satiric light. His view of satire contained in a letter to Pope on July 17, 1734, at the end of his career and only a few months before his death, reflects his career as a satirist:

And I make it my Last Request, that you continue that noble *Disdain* and *Abhorrence* of Vice, which you seem naturally endu'ed with, but still with a due regard to your own Safety; and study more to reform than to chastise, tho' the one cannot be effected without the other. [23]

This kind of satire is most evident in *The History of John Bull*, the work with which Arbuthnot is most often associated and which shows him at his best.

CHAPTER 3

The History of John Bull

W ITH the possible exception of Uncle Sam, John Bull is the best-known personification of a nation. Since his creation with the first of Arbuthnot's John Bull pamphlets in March 1712 and continuing over two and a half centuries, he has fascinated cartoonists and artists like James Gillray, Thomas Rowlandson, John Leech, Sir John Tenniel, and Thomas Nast, as well as writers such as George Colman the Younger, James Boswell, James K. Paulding, Washington Irving, James Russell Lowell, and Christy Brown.[1] Whenever and wherever the English presence is felt or seen, John Bull comes to mind: bluff, good-natured, hearty, at times bullying, but rarely cruel or deceitful.

The five pamphlets which created this enduring symbol appeared anonymously from March through July of 1712. Though an occasional scholar has been reluctant to assign them to Arbuthnot, the consensus leaves little reasonable doubt that they are his.[2] In tone, humor, and style they are consistent with Arbuthnot's other work and with his political views. Combined into *The History of John Bull*, published in 1727, the work is one of the two major satires with which Arbuthnot's name will always be rightfully associated and one which justifiably establishes him as a major English Satirist.

The history, however, is one of those occasional satires which must be read in the light of its historical context if its full meaning is to be enjoyed and the accomplishment of the satirist accurately measured. It is not necessary that a precise historical parallel be established for every detail or turn of the political and religious situations in England in the first fifteen years or so of the eighteenth century, but the reader must have an overview of the issues and personalities in order to appreciate what Arbuthnot is attempting to do.

The John Bull allegory is a complex fabric woven of materials drawn from English foreign and domestic affairs in the years from about 1700 to 1715. It touches upon the War of the Spanish Succession; the personalities and careers of the Duke of Marlborough, Queen Anne, Robert Harley (Oxford), Henry St. John (Bolingbroke), among others; the trial of the extremist Tory clergyman Henry Sacheverell; the Anglican-Dissenter agitation over the practice of occasional conformity; and the bitter division of the nation over the conduct of the war and the search for peace. Distant and obscure to most modern readers, these were the personalities and problems which irritated and frustrated England for over a decade, and involved Arbuthnot's closest friends. Arbuthnot and his contemporaries—whether Whig or Tory, Anglican, Dissenter, or Roman Catholic—were not only troubled by these issues, but they also held in the backs of their minds the memories of the political, religious, and social turbulence which had afflicted England throughout the preceding century and had sent one king (Charles I) to the executioner's block and another (James II) into exile. Thus, to make the allegory of Arbuthnot's major political satire more intelligible, a brief sketch of the historical background is necessary.

The war with France had begun in 1702 when a coalition formed by England, Austria, the Netherlands, and some of the small German principalities moved to prevent Louis XIV of France from upsetting the European balance of power as he attempted to put his grandson, Philip of Anjou, on the Spanish throne and thus unite the crowns of France and Spain.[3] The death of Charles II of Spain, childless and half-witted, brought about the start of hostilities. In England the Tories were doubtful of the wisdom and eventual success of an English military adventure on the Continent, but the brilliant victories of John Churchill, Duke of Marlborough, at Blenheim (1704), Ramillies (1706), Oudenarde (1708), and Malplaquet (1709) gave the English nation a temporary but heady feeling of eventual victory. Nevertheless, the cracks of domestic division began to appear as the moderate Tory coalition under Sidney Godolphin gradually became a Whig government dominated by Marlborough and his wife, Sarah Jennings, who was Queen Anne's closest advisor and confidante. In short, the war increasingly came to be viewed as a Whig cause; the heavy expense of the conflict (£1,250,000 in 1702 and £3,375,000 in 1709, for example)[4] fell mostly on the Tory landowners while the Whig middle class, who as businessmen filled the large military contracts and stood to gain from possible expansion of English colonialism, reaped huge profits. Generally speaking, the Tories were eager to end a war which they viewed as inimical to their own interests and those of the nation, while the Whigs, for reasons equally valid to their own way of thinking, wanted a peace which would require a more extended military effort.

After a sensible peace treaty offered by Louis in 1709 had been rejected, the Whig leadership was replaced by a Tory government led by Robert Harley, Earl of Oxford, and Henry St. John, Viscount Bolingbroke, who proceeded to negotiate a peace. The search for peace was complicated by the national furor over the passage of the Occasional Conformity Act of 1711, designed to prevent non-Anglicans from qualifying for certain public offices by merely taking an occasional communion in the Anglican mode, and over Sacheverell's denunciations of the Whig government in 1709 for its seeming indifference to the interests of the state church and his subsequent trial, which resulted in his three-year suspension from preaching and, ironically, the fall of his Whig antagonists in the government.

Peace finally came in 1713 with the Treaty of Utrecht, by which England gained Gibraltar and Minorca in the Mediterranean, and Nova Scotia, Newfoundland, and the Hudson Bay region in North America, as well as a share in the Spanish slave trade (the Asiento treaty, the violation of which by the Spaniards a quarter of a century later was to drag England into another war and hasten the fall of the powerful prime minister, Sir Robert Walpole). Philip of Anjou retained the throne of Spain as Philip V, but France and Spain promised never to unite their kingdoms. The French fortifications at Dunkirk were to be demolished, and the so-called "barrier fortresses" along the southern border of the Netherlands were to be manned by Dutch troops, thus providing some degree of security for the tiny nation.

The agitation over the war and the peace negotiations involved a large segment of the English literary community, including Addison, Defoe, Congreve, Gay, Matthew Prior, Pope, Swift, and Steele, either as propagandists and apologists or as political functionaries for one party or the other. But the peace brought only temporary respite from factionalism; Queen Anne died in 1714, and the Tory ministry of Oxford and Bolingbroke fell. Bolingbroke, impeached by Parliament, fled to France; Oxford and other Tories were indicted on trumped-up charges; and the Tories fell into such disarray and disrepute that they remained a much less powerful force in English politics for well over half a century.

In the midst of this continuing foreign and domestic crisis, Arbuthnot wrote and published his John Bull pamphlets in the spring and summer of 1712. *Law is a Bottomless Pit* appeared on March 6, *John Bull in His Senses* on March 18, *John Bull Still in His Senses* on April 17, *An Appendix to John Bull Still in His Senses* on May 9, and *Lewis Baboon Turned Honest* and *John Bull Politician* (published together but usually considered separately) on July 31. These were brought together, with a revision into two parts, in the second volume of the Pope-Swift *Miscellanies* of 1727.

The plot of *The History of John Bull* is a good deal simpler than the events which occasioned it. John Bull (England) joins with Nicholas Frog (the Dutch) and others in a lawsuit (the War of the Spanish Succession) against Philip Baboon (the Duke of Anjou), who is now Lord Strutt (Philip V, King of Spain. "Baboon" is a pun on "Bourbon," the name of the ruling families in Spain and France. Philip had obtained his livery (the right of succession to the Spanish throne) from Lewis Baboon (Louis XIV of France). But Bull and Frog claim by means of contracts to be the exclusive drapiers to the Strutt family. Goaded by his attorneys, chief among them Humphrey Hocus (John Churchill, Duke of Marlborough), Bull becomes enamored of the legal profession and retires from his business to become a lawyer, all the while dreaming of future profits and boasting of his legal abilities.

But Bull soon discovers a love affair between his wife (the Whig ministry) and Hocus. He quarrels with her; she is grievously injured in the encounter and, after treatment by quacks, dies (the fall of the Whigs and rise of the Tories) as she utters a curse that he will never come to peace with Strutt. She also leaves him the distracted father of three daughters: Polemnia (war), Discordia (political factionalism), and Usuria (financial chaos). Glad, as are his friends, that the old shrew is dead, he takes a wise second wife (the Tory ministry of Harley and St. John), who at first angers him by demanding that he forsake the law and return to his business. Looking over his account books and finding how he has been bilked by Hocus and Frog, he seeks the assistance of Sir Roger Bold (Harley) in hopes of withdrawing from the lawsuit. But he and his wife are frustrated in the efforts by the abuse of Don Diego (Nottingham, a dissident Tory), Hocus (who has now become the guardian of

Polemnia, war), and Esquire South (Austria), all of whom seek to prevent Bull's settlement of differences with Strutt and thus to protect their own selfish interests. The efforts of Bold and the Bulls are also complicated by the troubles of Bull's mother (the Church of England) with Bull's sister Peg (Scotland), Timothy Trim (Low-Church Anglicanism), and Signiora Bubonia (the Pope), as Peg refuses to give up her lover Jack (Calvinism).

The conflict is at length resolved at a conference at Salutation Tavern (Utrecht) with Bull, South, Frog, and Lewis Baboon, but their efforts toward a settlement are at first unsuccessful; Bull's family fears that he will not leave his estate to his nephew (the Elector of Hanover, who was to become George I of England after Anne's death in 1714). Bull opens private negotiations with Baboon and arrives at an accommodation with him by which Ecclesdown Castle (Dunkirk) is turned over to Bull. The remainder of the narrative, contained in *Lewis Baboon Turned Honest, and John Bull, Politician*, tells how Bull returns home to find his family in an uproar and how Bull and Frog settle their differences.

Putting down his pen in the summer of 1712, Arbuthnot could not foresee the fall of his Tory friends just two years later. Had he been able to do so, his satirical allegory might have taken on a much darker and more bitter cast; as it now stands the book is a rollicking, delightful, and memorable satire of English politics in the earlier eighteenth century which provided educated and concerned readers of the time with an amusing commentary on the intrigues of statesmen and nations. *The History of John Bull* deserves a low-priced edition for modern students, for the passions and methods of politicians and diplomats have changed little in the past two and a half centuries.

The satire of the *History* is characteristically Arbuthnot's—urbane, whimsical, without noticeable animus. Throughout the narrative he satirizes personalities, institutions, and professions in a vivid manner that would have made them recognizable to most readers of his day, particularly the educated men and women among whom satire has traditionally found its most receptive audience. The readers of the *Tatler* and the *Spectator*, accustomed to this sophisticated kind of satire, would have enjoyed John Bull and seen him as a member of the same family as Sir Roger de Coverley, Sir Andrew Freeport, and Mr. Spectator. Although the satire had little or no effect (as is usual with satire) upon the course of the war and the progress of the peace negotiations, there can be little doubt that it amused the Tories and discomfited the Whigs.

One of the most fascinating aspects of the *History* is a lively characterization which creates caricatures comparable to the best of Swift and Pope. Although most of the characters are types associated with the satiric tradition coming down from both Horace and Juvenal, and although they personify people, nations, and institutions associated with the war, John Bull himself is a memorable individual with great strengths (and some endearing flaws) of character. As Arbuthnot draws him in loving detail, he is, for the most part,

an honest, plain-dealing Fellow, Cholerick, Bold, and of a very unconstant Temper, he dreaded not Old *Lewis* either at Back-Sword, single Faulchion, or Cudgel-play; but then he was very apt to quarrel with his best Friends, especially if they pretended to govern him: If you flatter'd him, you might lead him like a Child. John's Temper depended very much upon the Air; his Spirits rose and fell with the Weather-glass.[5]

He is bright and astute in his business dealings, but careless in his accounting and often the easy victim of his servants, workers, and partners, in part because he is "a Boon Companion, loving his Bottle and his Diversion; for to say Truth, no Man kept a better House than *John*, nor spent his Money more generously" (p. 9). Obviously, Arbuthnot had some doubts about the huge subsidies that England was providing its allies.

But solid and convivial as he is, the exemplar of the traditional English virtues, he can also be gulled by his own pride and by those who know how to exploit both his strengths and weaknesses. At the hands of Hocus he squanders his fortune in a ten-year lawsuit in which he spares no expense:

there wanted not *Yellow-boys* to fee Counsel, hire Witnesses, and bribe Juries. . . . *John* was promis'd, That the next [verdict] and the next would be the final Determination; but alas! that final Determination, and happy Conclusion was like an inchanted Island, the nearer *John* came to it, the further it went from him: New Tryals upon new Points still arose; new Doubts, new Matters to be cleared; . . . *John's* ready Mony [*sic*], Book-Debts, Bonds, Mortgages, all went into the Lawyers Pockets; then *John* began to borrow Money upon *Bank-Stock*, *East-India* Bonds, now and then a Farm went to Pot. (pp. 10 - 11)

Bull's problems with the lawyers and his increasingly desperate financial straits represent the difficulties that the English government faced in trying to balance the interests of its allies (as well as England's own) with the demands of the military operations, the burgeoning cost of the war, and the attendant evils of inflation and corruption.

As his frustration and anger mount, he does not hesitate to vent his irritation on Strutt and Lewis Baboon, the former's servants often coming "home naked, without Shoes, Stockings, and Linnen," the latter "reduc'd to his last Shift, . . . his Children . . . reduc'd from rich Silks to *Doily* Stuffs, his Servants in Rags and bare-footed, instead of good Victuals, they now lived upon Neck-Beef and Bullocks-Liver" (p. 11). Thus, as the belligerents wear themselves out, the only ones who profit are the politicians, the military leaders, the bankers, and the war contractors.

Undaunted by his lack of success in the courts, John still dreams of legal eminence and its perquisites:

Bless me! What immense Estates these Fellows raise by the Law? Besides, it is the Profession of a Gentleman: What a Pleasure it is to be victorious in a Cause? To swagger at the Bar? What a Fool am I to drudge any more in this Woollen-Trade? for a Lawyer I was born, and a Lawyer I will be; one is never too Old to learn. (pp. 11 - 12)

He proceeds to loiter about the courts of justice, learns legal jargon "enough to conjure up the Devil," and spouts it so often in the presence of his fellow tradesmen that they begin to shun him: "Instead of the Affairs of *Blackwell-Hall*, and the Price of Broadcloth, Wool, and Bayses, he talk'd of nothing but *Actions upon the Case, Returns, Capias, Alias capias, Demurrers, Venire facias, Replevins, Superseda's, Certiorari's, Writs of Error, Actions of Trover and Conversion, Trespasses, Precipes & Dedimus*" (p. 12). Frog, on the other hand, minds his own cloth business while at the same time watching closely the course of the lawsuit. For Arbuthnot's readers, this Dutch wiliness in matters of war and trade must have confirmed their own suspicions.

Thus put upon and gulled by almost everyone else, Bull blunders his way through and eventually wins an accommodation. Arbuthnot succeeds in drawing him as an earnest, naive, and much-harassed victim of a pack of rogues. Frog is a "cunning sly Whoreson, quite the reverse of *John* in many Particulars: Covetous, Frugal; minded domestick Affairs; would pine his Belly to save his Pocket, never lost a Farthing by careless Servants, or bad Debtors: He did not care much for any sort of Diversions, except Tricks of *High German* Artists, and *Leger de main*; no Man exceded *Nic.* in these, yet it must be own'd, that *Nic.* was a fair Dealer, and in that way had acquir'd immense Riches" (p. 10). Arbuthnot's caricature of the Dutch draws heavily upon the eighteenth-century Englishman's stereotype of the lowlanders as emotionally cold, phlegmatic, dull, materialistic, and financially astute; to make his satire effective he counts heavily upon the increasing English resentment toward what appeared to be Dutch military and diplomatic intransigence.

Another rogue is Bull's attorney, Hocus, who serves to draw the lightning of Marlborough's enemies, whose numbers in the government and the military were almost legion. This military darling of the Whigs is

an old cunning Attorney, what he wanted of Skill in Law, was made up by a Clerk which he kept, that was the prettiest Fellow in the World; he lov'd Money, was smooth-tongu'd, gave good Words, and seldom lost his Temper: He was not worse than an Infidel; he provided plentifully for his Family, but he lov'd himself better than them all: He had a Termagant Wife, and, as the Neighbours said, was plaguy Hen-peck'd; he was seldom observ'd, as some Attornies will practice, to give his own personal Evidence in Causes; he rather chose to do it *per test. conduct.* in a word, the Man was very well for an Attorney. (p. 10)

In this short sketch, as well as in various episodes, Hocus-Marlborough emerges as a vain, avaricious, politically partisan and self-seeking villain who is perfectly willing (as the Tories, including Swift, believed) to accept political bribes of all sorts from the Whigs, including the magnificent Blenheim Palace, built by the architect-playwright Sir John Vanbrugh. His wife, Sarah Jennings, hated by many for her influence with the ailing queen, is treated roughly in the 1712 pamphlet, as seen above, but in the 1727 edition the passage is altered to describe Swift's old enemy as a "mild spirited Woman."[6]

As harsh and unfair to Marlborough as Arbuthnot's treatment is, it does not approach the bitterness of Swift's "Satirical Elegy on the Death of a Late Famous General" (1722), of which the following is a representative passage:

> This world he cumber'd long enough;
> He burnt his candle to the snuff;
> And that's the reason, some folks think,

> He left behind so great a s- - -k.
> Let pride be taught by this rebuke,
> How very mean a thing's a Duke;
> From all his ill-got honours flung,
> Turn'd to that dirt from whence he sprung.[7]

The treatments of Marlborough by Arbuthnot and Swift are just what one might expect from the politically partisan satirist, a writer who traditionally gives no quarter and expects none, who selects only those details which prove his case and ignores any matters in extenuation or mitigation. Fortunately for both the duke and his duchess, their careers and personalities have been treated more objectively by modern biographers such as Sir Winston Churchill (a descendant), Ivor F. Burton, and David Green.[8]

The satire is also occasionally directed at professions and institutions such as law and medicine, Scots Presbyterianism, and Calvinism. All of these are common satirical targets in the eighteenth century, but Arbuthnot's laughter at their expense is often gentler than that of Samuel Butler, William Wycherley, or Swift.

The lawyers are shown as materialistic, corrupt, and proud.[9] When Bull decides to dismiss Hocus and hire Bold instead, he is berated by South, Frog, Ned the Chimney-Sweeper (Duke of Savoy), and Tom the Dust-man (Peter II, King of Portugal). And Mrs. Hocus, angrily breathing some of the best billingsgate Arbuthnot could write, confronts Mrs. Bull:

You silly, aukward, ill-bred, Country Sow you, have you no more Manners than to rail at my Husband, that has sav'd that Clod-pated, Numskull'd Ninny-hammer of yours from Ruin, and all his Family? it is well known how he has rose early and sate up late to make him easy, when he was Sotting at every Alehouse in Town. (p. 19)

She then proceeds to insult the appearance of this (the second) Mrs. Bull by comparison with that of her predecessor:

I knew his last Wife, she was a Woman of breeding, good humour, and complaisance, knew how to live in the World; as for you, you look like a Puppet mov'd by Clock-work; your Cloaths hang upon you, as they were upon Tenter-hooks, and you come into a Room as you were going to steal away a Piss-pot. (p. 19)

But all of this is merely a prologue to her defense of the career of her attorney-husband, of whom she proudly claims that he "has an establish'd Reputation, he never swore an Oath, nor told a Lie in all his Life; He is grateful to his Benefactors, faithful to his Friends, liberal to his Dependants, and dutiful to his Superiours; he values not your Money more than the Dust under his Feet, but he hates to be abus'd" (p. 19). To an audience that knew Marlborough's reputation and the tribe of lawyers, this passage must have been delightful.

The lawyers also try to intimidate Bull by spreading reports that he and his wife are mad, that he goes without shoes and stockings, that he does nothing but beat his servants, that Mrs. Bull is a "natural"—an idiot. And thus John often finds his house "beset with a whole Regiment of Attorneys Clerks, Bailiff and Bailiff-Followers, and other small retainers of the Law, who threw Stones at his Windows, and Dirt at himself, as he went along the Street" (p. 20).

Arbuthnot's satire on law is perhaps at its finest in the first chapter of the second pamphlet, *John Bull in His Senses*, where the first Mrs. Bull rationalizes her adultery with Hocus in a paper found by the cuckolded Bull. The incident allegorizes the Tory speeches in defense of Dr. Henry Sacheverell at his famous trial for libel in early 1710,[10] but it is also a brilliant parody of legal reasoning. Mrs. Bull argues that marriage is founded upon a contract by which the wife gives over her natural rights to her husband. But, she claims, the obligation is reciprocal: when the contract is broken, it ceases to have any power over the injured party, whose own redress is "that Original Right, or rather that indispensable Duty of Cuckoldom, lodg'd in all Wives" (p. 25). Citing precedence of both custom and law, Mrs. Bull reasons that the right of cuckoldry is compatible with the law of nature and that to "assert the Illegality of Cuckoldom, upon any Pretence whatsoever, were to cast odious Colours upon the married State, to blacken the necessary Means of perpetuating Families: . . . to defeat the very end of Matrimony, the Propagation of Mankind" (p. 26). To insist upon a wife's fidelity, she says, "strikes at the Root, digs the Foundation, and removes the Basis upon which the Happiness of a married State is built" (p. 27). And thus Bull, so enamored of legal quibbling himself, finds himself defeated by his own devices. But Arbuthnot was not done with the lawyers; he would return to them in Chapter XV of *The Memoirs of*

Martinus Scriblerus, as we shall see in the next chapter.

But although Arbuthnot has a great deal of fun with his satire of the lawyers, he does not let his own profession go unscathed. Devoted as he was to the art of healing and as proficient and respected as he was in it, he knew that it was sometimes practiced by charlatans and incompetents. Thus in Chapter IX of the first pamphlet, after the first Mrs. Bull has received a bruise in the right side in her fight with her husband, she is attended by Signior Cavallo (Charles Seymour, Sixth Duke of Somerset), "an Italian Quack" who claims to have "an infallible Ointment and Plaister" as well as a pill "that would purge off all her bad Humours, sweeten her Blood, and rectifie her disturb'd Imagination." But she just grows worse—"every Day she stank so no Body durst come within a Stone's throw of her, except Signior *Cavallo* and his Wife"—and the quack pretends to everyone that she is growing better, "that she should dance a Jig next *October* in *Westminster Hall*." But at last his quackery is exposed:

At last Signior one Day was sent for in great haste, his Patient growing worse and worse; when he came he affirmed, that it was a gross Mistake, that she was never in a fairer way: Bring hither the Salve, says he, and give her a plentiful Draught of my Cordial. As he was applying his Ointments, and administring the Cordial, the Patient gave up the Ghost, to the great Confusion of Signior *Cavallo*, and the great Joy of *Bull* and his Friends. Signior flung away out of the House in great disorder, and swore there was foul Play, for he was sure his Medicines were infallible. (p. 15)

Thus Cavallo (with all of the horse-doctor implications of his name) and his bungling arts, his chicanery, his incompetence, and his stupidity remind us of Swift's attacks upon physicians and panaceas in *A Tale of a Tub* and *Gulliver's Travels*, though the satire in both of Swift's works is at once both more sweeping and more bitter. Arbuthnot's satire is the more amusing, perhaps, for having been written by one who took pride in his profession while at the same time being objective enough to recognize its occasional failings.

Equally interesting is the satire directed against the religious difficulties of the period. The troubles among Anglicans, Dissenters, and Roman Catholics were hardly of recent origin in 1712, and certainly in the literature of the Restoration and the early eighteenth century there were strong appeals for religious moderation by John Locke, the Latitudinarians, and the Deists. But as long as Dissenters and Catholics lay under the political, religious, and social disenfranchisement of the Clarendon Code (1661 - 1665) and the Test Act (1673), despite some amelioration of their condition by the Act of Toleration (1689) and some loosened enforcement of the laws, they continued to agitate for a removal of the provisions of the Test. Some of the less tender consciences had evaded the Test by periodically taking communion as an Anglican, but this kind of evasion came increasingly under attack by churchmen and politicians who wanted to stop the practice of "occasional conformity."

But there were also fears on the part of Anglicans and Dissenters regarding the threat of the Pretender, James, son of the deposed James II. The unpleasant memories of the declarations of indulgence under Charles II and the subsequent attempts at exclusion bills in the late 1670s and early 1680s, the Popish Plot of 1678, the rebellion of the Duke of Monmouth in 1685 (events forming the background for Dryden's *Absalom and Achitophel* and *The Medal*), and the uncertainties surrounding the deposing of James II in 1688 - 1689—all these were very much in the minds of the English people.

Unlike his friend Swift, who entered the religious controversies as early as 1704 with the publication of *A Tale of a Tub* and its scalding satire of Puritan enthusiasm and Catholic superstition (with a few jabs at Anglicanism itself), Arbuthnot stayed clear of religious satire until he issued the John Bull pieces, and even then he avoided the more rancorous aspects of the issues.

The religious satire occurs in the third pamphlet, *John Bull Still in His Senses*. John Bull's mother, who represents the Anglican Church, is portrayed as a grave, sober, discreet, virtuous woman; she is not a Puritan ("one of your precise *Prudes*") or a Catholic ("one of your phantastical old *Belles*, that dress themselves like Girls of Fifteen"). Having foresworn the trappings of Romanism—ruffs, high-crowned hats, feathers, flowers, hooped petticoats, patches, and paint—she lives a simple life but is "not asham'd of a Diamond Cross." Her manner is genteel, and she is "well-bred without Affectation, in the due mean between one of your affected Curtsying pieces of Formality, and your Romps that have no regard to the common Rules of Civility" (p. 48). Mother Bull thus emerges as a symbol of Anglicanism, the moderate *via media* between the "precise *Prudes*" and "Romps" of Dissent and the "phantastical old *Belles*" and curtsying "pieces of Formality" of Catholicism.

But Mother Bull is also the target of those who want to drive a wedge between her and her son; indeed they had already been successful once in doing so (the Civil Wars and the Interregnum, 1642 - 1660): "he turn'd her out of Doors to his great Sorrow, as he found afterwards, for his Affairs went all at sixes and sevens" (p. 49). She remains judicious and studious, preaches chastity and conjugal fidelity (passive obedience to the government), but never delivers her teachings with "dogmatical Assertions, *This is infallible; I cannot be mistaken; none but a Rogue can deny it*" (p. 49).

Arbuthnot thus establishes Anglicanism as a comfortable middle way between the formalism, ceremony, and superstition of Catholicism and the doctrinal fanaticism and creed-spawning theology of the Dissenters, both groups sharing a great amount of arrogance and intolerance. Mother Bull serves pretty much the same function as Martin in Swift's *Tale of a Tub* and Dryden himself in *Religio Laici*; she serves to show that the Anglican Church offered to Arbuthnot's contemporaries a type of Christianity compatible with the history, institutions, temperament, and destiny of the English nation. Like many of his fellows Arbuthnot looked back over a century and a half of religious wrangling which had too often spilled out of the pulpit into the political conflicts and social disruptions of (as Swift put it in Book I of *Gulliver's Travels*, with some hyperbole) "six Rebellions . . . wherein one Emperor lost his Life, and another his Crown."[11]

The spiritual tranquility of John and his mother is soon disturbed by his sister Peg, who represents both the nation and the church of Scotland. But unlike the plump John, she looks starved:

and no wonder, for *John* was the Darling, he had all the good Bits, was cramm'd with good Pullet, Chicken, Pig, Goose, and Capon; while Miss had only a little Oatmeal and Water, or a dry Crust without Butter. *John* had his golden Pippens, Peaches and Nectarnes; poor Miss had a Crab-Apple, Sloe or a Blackberry. Master lay in the best Apartment, with his Bed-Chamber toward the South-Sun. Miss lodg'd in a Garret, expos'd to the North-Wind, which shrevel'd her countenance; however, this Usage tho' it stunted the Girl in her Growth, gave her a hardy Constitution; she had Life and Spirit in abundance, and knew when she was ill used. (p. 50)

Peg and John are continually squabbling; at times their confrontations end in violence and name-calling—"she call'd him *Gundy-Guts*, and he call'd her *Lousy-Peg*" (p. 50). But even more irritating to John is the courtship of Peg by a scabrous suitor named Jack (Calvinism).

The *Jack* of the John Bull pamphlet is a close relative of his namesake in Swift's *Tale of a Tub*; he has "a most scandalous Tongue" and accuses all other suitors (religious groups) of being "pox'd by that scarlet-fac'd Whore *Signiora Bubonia*"—Peter (Catholicism), for example, is covered with venereal scabs, and Martin (Anglicanism or Lutheranism) has nocturnal pains of an erotic origin (p. 51). Jack pretends to be "the only Man in the World, of a sound, pure, and untainted Constitution" but is suspected of carrying on a hidden intrigue with the Pope. He is also charged with being a swindler, a fop, a hypocrite, a cantankerous spirit who "would cry at a Wedding, laugh and make Jests at a Funeral," eat roast beef during a fast and gruel when allowed to eat his fill (pp. 51 - 52).

Jack's political and scientific theories are as absurd as his religious doctrines. He believes, for example, that "All Government . . . is founded upon the right Distribution of Punishments; decent Executions keep the World in awe; for that Reason, the majority of Mankind ought to be hang'd every Year" (p. 52). Furthermore, he thinks that certain children should be reared to crime so that their executions might serve as examples to the rest of mankind. And in science his favorite theories are "exploded Chimeras, the *perpetuum Mobile*, the circular Shot, Philosopher's Stone, and silent Gunpowder, making chains for Fleas, Nets for Flies, and Instruments to unravel cobwebs, and split Hairs" (p. 53).

In one way or another Arbuthnot employs most of the old suspicions about Puritans that had found their way into literature from the time of Shakespeare and Jonson down to the early eighteenth century: their fanatic hatred of Catholicism, their insistence upon rigid doctrinal purity, their violent attacks upon the theology of other Christians, their peculiarities in dress and diet, their aversions to church art, and their theories of education.[12] None of these satiric shots is original with Arbuthnot, and a reading of the passages recalls the same kinds of anti-Puritan charges made in Samuel Butler's *Hudibras* (1663, 1664, 1668) and Swift's *Tale of a Tub*, to name only the more obvious. Somehow, though, Arbuthnot does not pursue Jack with the same bitterness that Swift devoted to his own Jack or that Butler lavished upon the Presbyterian Hudibras and his Independent squire, Ralpho. Time and again in this satire and others Arbuthnot avoided taking advantage of opportunities for more pungent ridicule.

John Bull, of course, cannot understand what Peg sees in Jack and views him as a fit husband for only the daughter of a shoemaker or tailor, but Peg will have nothing to do with any of her brother's eligible friends, "your flaunting Beaus, that gang with their Breasts open, and their Sarks over their Waistcoats, that accost me with set Speeches out of *Sidney's Arcadia*, or *The Academy of Compliments*." She much prefers Jack, whom she thinks an excellent marriage prospect—sober, grave, sincere, and pious (pp. 53 - 54).

But if Peg is a wrongheaded daughter, she is also an industrious woman who preserves her pride and the respect of her neighbors. She makes her way in the world by selling knives, scissors, fish, and shoebuckles, and by spinning and knitting; and "in these her poor Circumstances, she still preserv'd the Air and Mien of a Gentlewoman; a certain decent Pride, that extorted Respect from the haughtiest of her Neighbours" (p. 54). Eventually John comes to an accommodation with her in his will, which collectively symbolizes the Act of Toleration (1689, giving Dissenters freedom of worship), the Act of Settlement (1701), and the union of England and Scotland (1707). Thus,

by the Interposition of good Friends, and by many a bonny thing that were sent, and many more that were promis'd *Peg*, the Matter was concluded, and *Peg* taken into the House upon certain Articles; one of which was, That she might have the Freedom of *Jack's* Conversation, and might take him for Better and for Worse, if she pleas'd; provided always, he did not come into the House at unseasonable Hours, and disturb the Rest of the Old Woman, *John's* Mother. (p. 55)

This appeasement of Peg brings John no real peace, for he must still quiet the eccentric Jack. Old Mrs. Bull falls ill, as John tells his wife, of "an odd sort of a Distemper; it began with a Coldness and Numbness in her Limbs, which by degrees affected the Nerves . . . seized the Brain, and at last ended in a Lethargy" (p. 66). She becomes violent, is hard with her servants, and squanders her money on bullies. Sir Roger Bold and the physicians (among them Samuel Garth) try to cure her by a variety of measures including bloodletting and purges. But one of her liverymen, Yan Ptschirnsooker (Bishop Gilbert Burnet), has been giving her a powder which, he says,

*does temperate de Humour, despel de Windt, and cure de Vapour; it
lulleth and quieteth de Animal Spirits, procuring Rest, and pleasant
Dreams: It is de infallible Receipt for de Scurvy, all Heats in de Bloodt, and
Breaking out upon de Skin; It is de true Bloodt Stancher, stopping all Flux-
es of de Bloodt. If you take dis, you will never ail any ding; it will Cure you
of all Diseases.* (p. 69)

Since Jack is found to be the plotter of all the schemes against
Mother Bull, a hue and cry is raised against him, and he is brought
to trial for various crimes: stockjobbing, consorting with low
women, and getting into office by occasional conformity (pp. 78 -
81 *passim*).

In jail he is visited by Habakkuk Slyboots (Lord Somers),
who persuades him that he would be best advised to let himself be
hanged and then rescued by Sir Roger, who will cut him down
before he is dead. Jack is indeed hanged, but Sir Roger is all too
willing to let him die: "Then let him hang. I don't wonder at it, the
Fellow has been mad these twenty Years" (p. 87). Jack, however, is
not dead: "*Jack*, after all, had some small Tokens of Life in him, but
lies at this time past hopes of a total Recovery, with his Head hanging upon one Shoulder, without Speech or Motion. The Coroners
Inquest supposing him Dead, brought him in *Non Compos*" (p. 87).

In this episode of Mother Bull's difficulties with Jack and his con-
sequent near-execution, Arbuthnot burlesques the continuing controversy over occasional conformity. As the Dissenters gained financial and political influence, they increasingly agitated to have the
Test Act of 1673 repealed or modified so that they might hold
political office without having to compromise their consciences by
taking annual communion in an Anglican chapel. The controversy
was dividing Englishmen along religious lines just at a time when
the war and the peace negotiations were also raising partisan
emotions to their highest. Among Swift's literary contemporaries,
Swift and Defoe were deeply involved in the debate, Swift with,
among other pieces, *A Letter Concerning the Sacramental Test*
(1708) and *An Argument against Abolishing Christianity* (1708),
Defoe as early as 1698 and 1702 with an *Enquiry into the Occasional Conformity of the Dissenters* and *The Shortest Way with
Dissenters*, the latter getting him into legal difficulties and sending
him to the pillory. As early as 1702 an occasional conformity bill was
introduced in Parliament to punish those who, having taken the
prescribed communion, went on to fill offices in the municipalities,
the armed forces, the Parliament, or the national government, and

then continued to attend Dissenter religious services. Subsequently the bill was brought up several more times but failed. Finally, at the urging of the Earl of Nottingham (Don Diego) and Lord Somers (Slyboots) the bill was introduced a fourth time, with clauses to broaden religious toleration. Some of the Whigs were persuaded to support the bill with the implied promise that Harley (Sir Roger Bold) would find a way to have it thrown out. The Occasional Conformity Act, however, passed in 1711, and the Dissenters were no better off than before.[13]

Thus *The History of John Bull* is an allegorical montage of events, issues, and personalities from the tumultuous scene from about 1700 to 1712, a period in which the other important writers of the time—Addison, Steele, Defoe, and Swift—were involved in the day-to-day matters of foreign and domestic politics. There is perhaps no other period of English or American literature when the major literary men were so much involved in political affairs; Addison was a Secretary of State, Steele a member of Parliament, Defoe and Swift party journalists. Arbuthnot, though hardly as combative as Steele and Swift, nevertheless took up his pen in hopes of restoring a degree of common sense to the scene while at the same time indulging his love of irony at the expense of those men and nations caught in the toils of a nagging and unpopular war.

The book is a mixed success. Arbuthnot is good at drawing lively and engaging caricatures. John Bull has become the symbol of the English spirit, a symbol so successful that he almost immediately occasioned a number of imitations and continuations by hands other than Arbuthnot's.[14] Ten pamphlets, all of them taking the Whig side of the issues, appeared in the next five years—two in 1713, five in 1714, one in 1715, and two in 1717—and in the second half of the century as well as the first part of the nineteenth there were other imitations in both England and America.

The particular aspects of the allegory may be lost upon the modern reader, but *The History of John Bull* still provides delightful reading for students of satire. Though never as urbane as the *Tatler* and the *Spectator*, or as graphic and biting as the satires of Pope, or as probing as the comic works of Swift, the history exhibits the work of a lively wit, an ironically observing eye, and a moral concern in a group of zestful character sketches, a robust and racy dialogue, and a free and whimsical tone.

With Dryden's *Absalom and Achitophel*, Swift's *Gulliver's*

Travels, and Samuel Butler's *Hudibras*, *The History of John Bull* belongs to the great tradition of eighteenth-century political and religious satire.

CHAPTER 4

The Memoirs of Martinus Scriblerus

T HE difficult years in which Arbuthnot was most deeply involved with current affairs—the years which saw the publication of the *John Bull* pamphlets and *The Art of Political Lying* and in which he was most active as one of the queen's physicians—were also those in which he was closest to Swift, Pope, and Gay, the other leading members of the little group most commonly known in literary history as the Scriblerus Club.

It was amid this circle of Augustan wits that Arbuthnot began his work as a satirist of pedantry, which culminated in *The Memoirs of Martinus Scriblerus* (eventually published many years later, in 1741, by Pope), which will be the subject of this chapter. His satire on learning is also to be found in *Three Hours after Marriage* (1717), a farce upon which he collaborated with Gay and Pope; in *Virgilius Restauratus* (1729), a burlesque of classical scholarship; in *A Brief Account* of *Mr. John Ginglicutt's Treatise* (1731), an attack upon false tastes in argumentation; and in *An Essay Concerning the Origin of Sciences* (1732), a parody of certain ingenious fashions in historical studies. These latter four works will be considered in Chapter 5.

I   *"The Clever Fellows"*

The small group which produced the *Memoirs* were, to the mind of the late eighteenth-century poet William Cowper, "the most celebrated collection of clever fellows this country ever saw." [1] All of them—Swift, Gay, Pope, Arbuthnot, Parnell, and Harley—were in their intellectual and professional maturity and had arrived at prominence in writing or public affairs. The formation of the club was the coming-together of men with similar tastes and interests, and their collaboration brought together their diverse skills and backgrounds into the production of one of the most entertaining

68

satires of false learning in the eighteenth century, a book which reflected not only their amusement at the trivialities of contemporary scholarship but also their fears as to the future of learning.

In late 1713 Pope suggested to Gay that they and some of their friends work together on a monthly periodical in which they would satirize excesses and follies in learning and criticism by means of ironic reviews thhat would ridicule learned works of genuine merit and praise the works of the fraternity of Grub Street writers.[2] He had earlier advanced this plan in a letter to Addison and Steele's *Spectator;* he proposed to publish a monthly *"Account of the Works of the Unlearned,"* a project in which he had been encouraged by recent works "of my own Country-men, who many of them make a very Eminent Figure in the Illiterate World." He says also that he will "take into Consideration such Pieces as appear, from time to time, under the Names of those Gentlemen who Complement one another in Public Assemblies, by the title of *Learned Gentlemen."* There will be an abundance of subject matter because:

Our Party-Authors will also afford me a great Variety of Subjects, not to mention Editors, Commentators, and others, who are often Men of no Learning, or what is as bad, of no Knowledge. I shall not enlarge upon this Hint; but if you think any thing can be made of it, I shall set about it with all the Pains and Application that so useful a Work deserves.[3]

But because of other considerations, political as well as literary, Pope did little about putting his plan into action. As Charles Kerby-Miller believes, Pope was too young and inexperienced at age twenty-four to carry off the project by himself.[4]

In the autumn of 1713, however, he approached Addison, Congreve, Parnell, Swift, and Francis Atterbury, Bishop of Rochester, with his proposal, but the group which finally gathered to work on the project included, instead, Pope, Swift, Gay, Arbuthnot, Parnell, and occasionally Harley. Just how this group was transformed into a club is not certain, but it began meeting as such about the end of the Christmas season. For the most part its meetings seem to have been informal ones held in the lodgings of its members, most often in Arbuthnot's room in St. James's Palace, where he lived in order to be close to the ailing queen. That the fellowship was social as well as intellectual is evident in an invitation to Harley probably written by Swift:

The Doctor and Dean, Pope, Parnell and Gay,
In manner submissive most humbly do pray,
That your Lordship would once let your Cares all
    Alone
And climb the dark Stairs to your Friends who
    have none:
To your Friends who at least have no Cares but
    to please you
To a good honest Junta that never will tease you.
         From the Doctor's Chamber
         past eight.[5]

The group was diverse in its interests and accomplishments. Swift had already published *The Battle of the Books* and *A Tale of a Tub*, as well as a host of other prose works and poems; Pope had seen his *Pastorals, The Rape of the Lock,* and *An Essay on Criticism* emerge in print. Gay had not started as well and had only *Rural Sports* and some lesser things to his credit; Parnell, who would die before the age of forty in 1718, had contributed to periodicals and miscellanies. Harley, obviously, was very much involved in domestic and political affairs, especially those involving the aftermath of the Peace of Utrecht. Thus the little circle not only included men who had made their mark but also a physician (Arbuthnot), two clergymen (Swift and Parnell), a politician (Harley), and two professional men of letters (Gay and Pope), each of whom would have something to contribute to the satire.

The business of the meetings was probably to establish the project and to discuss the proposals and drafts brought forward by the members, most of the actual writing being done between the meetings. For one reason or another, the club did not settle down to the arduous task of bringing these fragments together, and the various bits and pieces began to accumulate.

As they worked, the members found their objects of satire proliferating as each pursued his own interest. The scope of the satiric plan came eventually to cover the follies of philosophers, pedagogues, lawyers, physicians, critics, editors, artists, antiquarians, and even dancing-masters. The obvious need, then, was for some sort of vehicle to give unity and continuity to these disparate materials, and the final scheme seems to have been to develop a full biography of a pedant-hero and to present him to their readers in order to create a background for later projects, to publish further works under his name, and to attribute to him real experiments, projects, and publications. This plan gave the Scriblerians a wide range for their satire and provided them with several options in terms of form.

And thus Martinus Scriblerus (literally, Martin the Scribbler) was born, the son of a pedant and the friend of another, a dolt who can by turns be naive and sensible. Having created their central figure, the Scriblerians then set out to bring together materials suitable for the project, ranging far and wide in ancient and modern history, literature, philosophy, and science for ideas and supporting details.

The club, however, continued its work for only a few months in the late winter and spring; by June the group had disbanded for the summer, and the death of Queen Anne in August hastened the dispersal of the members and the end of the club as a functioning entity. Other business also drew the collaborators apart. Arbuthnot was increasingly involved in his medical attendance upon the queen; Pope was more and more engrossed in his translation of the *Iliad;* Harley was immersed in his political responsibilities and the disintegration of his ministry with Bolingbroke; Gay was finishing his *Shepherd's Week* and supervising its publication (April 15). Thus the project was set aside; the regular meetings of the club ended, and its project was never revived on any meaningful scale, though there were to be periodic attempts at its resurrection. After the summer of 1714 the influence of Scriblerus is largely to be seen in such individual works as Gay, Pope, and Arbuthnot's *Three Hours after Marriage* (1717), Swift's *Gulliver's Travels* (1726), and Pope's *Dunciad* (1728 *et seq.*), all of which drew to some degree upon the Scriblerian materials and traditions.

II *Authorship*

The major critical problem with *The Memoirs of Martinus Scriblerus* is assigning authorship of various portions of the book to individual Scriblerians. Determination of their parts in the composition of the work is complex and puzzling; about all that can be safely said is that the book as it finally emerged in the second volume of Pope's works in 1741 is a montage of ideas and stretches of writing by various members. Perhaps the best discussion of the authorship question is that by Kerby-Miller, but even his conclusions, as carefully and judiciously drawn as they are, must be accepted as only tentative.

But Arbuthnot's role was a major and important one. Swift, in writing to him on July 3, 1714, remarks:

To talk of Martin in any hands but yours, is a Folly. You every day give better hints than all of us together could do in a twelvemonth; And to say the Truth, Pope, who first thought of the Hint has no Genius at all to it, in my Mind. Gay is too young; Parnel has some Ideas in it, but is idle; I could putt together, and lard, and strike out well enough, but all that relates to the Sciences must be from you.[6]

This passage should not be read, as it might be tempting to do, to suggest that Arbuthnot wrote the whole of the *Memoirs*; as Kerby-Miller says, "His ability to produce suggestions is not to be confused with actual authorship. The task of building his clever suggestions into completed sections of the *Memoirs* fell largely to others."[7] Thus,

Not much can be done in the way of dividing the authorship of chapters among the Scriblerians according to special interests or knowledge. All the Scriblerians were very well educated and widely informed; hence, with the exception of the parts dealing with science, which are probably to be credited principally to the doctor, most of the *Memoirs* might have been written by any one or any combination of the Scriblerians.[8]

Kerby-Miller's conclusions are that much of Chapter Seven, which deals with logic and metaphysics, and Chapter Twelve (on freethinking) belongs to Arbuthnot and Parnell, but that beyond this little is certain, though "Dr. Arbuthnot's family of growing children and his lifelong interest in music may lead us to suspect that he was chiefly responsible for the fourth, fifth, and sixth chapters, which deal with education, playthings, and music."[9]

Thus we must be careful in reading the *Memoirs* to keep in mind that the points of satire and the narratives around them may not be specifically Arbuthnot's, but rather concerns which were as much his as those of his collaborators and which he saw as deserving of satiric treatment.

III   *The Satire on Learning*

The issue of authorship aside, *The Memoirs of Martinus Scriblerus* offers a fascinating view not only of the major intellectual interests of the Scriblerians but also an insight into Arbuthnot's own thinking, for there is little in the book with which he would not have sympathized. The satiric project was a serious one; the Scriblerians looked about them at a world in which much of the

learned community had seemingly run mad, when the age seemed
to be afflicted with a plague of virtuosi, quacks, pedants, and intellectual charlatans. Witnessing as they did the great political,
religious, social, and intellectual ferment of the early eighteenth
century, and motivated by their Tory and Anglican conservatism,
the Scriblerians struck out at all aberrations in learning and the
vestiges of corrupted wisdom from the past. It was an age in which
the popular acceptance of astrology, alchemy, and witchcraft,
though steadily waning, was still evident; when classical learning
was still freighted with loads of learned lumber; when the
educational system (as always) was failing to keep up with a fast-
moving and rapidly changing world. The Scriblerians looked upon
the scene with both humor and dismay; they were beginning to
view their world with a sense of increasing disillusionment that
would find its most despairing summation in the final line of Pope's
Dunciad : "And Universal Darkness buries All." [10]

In the "Introduction to the Reader" of *The Memoirs of the Extraordinary Life, Works, and Discoveries of Martinus Scriblerus* (the
full title), the narrator sets his scene in the reign of Queen Anne
(thus making certain that the historical point of his satire will not be
lost) and introduces us to his hero, "a certain Venerable Person"
who spends much of his time outside St. James's Palace and is
thought to be a "decay'd Gentleman of Spain." There is something
of Don Quixote in his haunted visage and his melancholy:

His stature was tall, his visage long, his complexion olive, his brows were
black and even, his eyes hollow yet piercing, his nose inclin'd to aquiline,
his beard neglected and mix'd with grey: All this contributed to spread a
solemn Melancholy over his countenance. Pythagoras was not more silent,
Pyrrho more motionless, nor Zeno more austere. His Wig was as black and
smooth as the plumes of a Raven, and hung as strait as the hair of a River-
God rising from the water. His Cloak so completely covered his whole person, that whether or no he had any other cloaths (much less any linen) under it, I shall not say; but his sword appear'd a full yard behind him, and
his manner of his wearing it was so stiff, that it seem'd grown to his Thigh.
His whole figure was so utterly unlike any thing of this world, that it was
not natural for any man to ask him a question without blessing himself first.
Those who never saw a *Jesuit* took him for one, and others believed him
some *High Priest of the Jews*. [11]

The man is mysterious, suspicious, sinister but also proud, half-
starved, and poverty-stricken. A manuscript in Latin drops from his

pocket, and is picked up and brought to the narrator, who, amazed at its contents, returns it to its melancholy owner, hears briefly the reasons for the stranger's past and present lamentable history, and is appointed his biographer, whereupon the ominous creature departs, never to be seen again (pp. 91 - 93).

The awesome man is, of course, Martinus Scriblerus, whose life and works are now to be revealed as the narrator moves to fulfill his promise: "I think it a debt no longer to be delay'd, to reveal what I know of this Prodigy of Science, and to give the History of his life, and of his extensive merits, to mankind; in which I dare promise the Reader, that, whenever he begins to think any one Chapter dull, the style will be immediately changed in the next" (p. 94). The last clause seems to be the narrator's device for covering the differences in style of materials contributed by members of the club.

The remainder of the book consists of seventeen chapters which relate the parentage, birth, education, adventures, travels, and works of Martin, together with an appended page listing "Pieces of Scriblerus (written in his youth) already published" and "Others not yet published, mentioned in the Memoirs." At times disjointed and underdeveloped, and at times failing to dramatize episodes rich in possibilities, the narrative bumps along at a broken pace as it carries its somewhat picaresque hero to the point at which the narrator meets him and learns his history.

We learn in Chapter I that Martin is the son of Cornelius Scriblerus, whose genealogy is traced on "a Skin of the true Pergamenian Parchment" from the period of the elder Pliny (first century A.D.) and including Albertus Magnus, Paracelsus, and the Scaligers, all of them well known in the early eighteenth century as examples of corrupt learning (p. 96). We are also told that Cornelius has been married to a beautiful woman in an idyllic union which has, unfortunately, proven barren simply because the old pedant "never had cohabitation with his spouse, but he ponder'd on the Rules of the Ancients, for the generation of Children of Wit," thus confining himself and his wife to a first-year's diet of goat's milk and honey in keeping with an ancient prescription for assuring pregnancy. His wife eventually conceives but miscarries in the fourth month. Cornelius is not particularly saddened, for "the Abortion proved only a female Foetus, . . . his heart being wholly fixed upon the learned Sex." Truly pedantic, he puts the fetus in a jar and places it among the curiosities of his family" (pp. 95 - 96).

But she conceives again, "to his unexpressible joy," and they go to London, where she inherits the estate of her Jewish uncle, and there Martin is born. In the period before the lad's birth Cornelius continues to live by all sorts of *a priori* schemes for the rearing of a boy; he had "already chalked out all possible schemes for the improvement of a male child; yet was so far prepar'd for the worst that could happen, that before the nine months were expired, he had composed two Treatises of Education; the one he called *A Daughter's Mirrour,* and the other *A Son's Monitor*" (p. 97), titles which the Scriblerians could count on to evoke a comic response in an audience at times inundated in a flood of books dealing with the proper rearing of children. The mother is all the while entertained with a daily musical concert in keeping, as Cornelius would have it, with the practice of the Magi (p. 97).

The boy finally enters the world in the slum district of St. Giles, his birth attended by a series of wonderful portents. Mrs. Scriblerus, on the night before delivery, dreams that she has given birth to a large, streaming inkhorn (which the alternately fanciful and unimaginative Cornelius interprets to mean that the child will be a "very voluminous Writer"). A barren crabtree proves fruitful (assuring "acuteness of Wit"); a swarm of wasps hovers around his crib without stinging him (presaging, says Cornelius, his satiric power); and a manure pile overnight sprouts mushrooms. Most significantly,

a monstrous *Fowl* . . . dropt through the sky-light, near his wife's apartment. It had a large body, two little disproportioned wings, a prodigious tail, but no head. As its colour was white, he took it at first sight for a Swan, and was concluding his son would be a Poet; but on a nearer view, he perceived it to be speckled with black, in the form of letters; and that it was indeed a Paper kite which had broke its leash by the impetuosity of the wind. His back was armed with the Art Military, his belly was filled with Physick, his wings were the wings of Quarles and Withers, the several Nodes of his voluminous tail were diversify'd with several branches of science; where the Doctor beheld with great joy a knot of Logick, a knot of Metaphysick, a knot of Casuistry, a knot of Polemical Divinity, and a knot of Common Law, with a *Lanthorn* of *Jacob Behmen.* (pp. 98 - 99)

And at his birth the boy is reported to have made the sounds of a calf, a magpie a hog, a colt, a raven, a cat, a goose, and an ass (p. 99).

The narrator thus, in his detailing of these omens, plays upon various clasical allusions to events surrounding the births of Homer and Virgil, Arbuthnot's own making of kites for his children, the emblematic poetry of Francis Quarles and George Wither, and the "inner light" doctrines of various seventeenth-century mystics, including the Quakers.[12] The references not only are comic in their twists upon older traditions, but also foreshadow the pedantic career of the boy.

Upon Martin's birth Cornelius is proud and arrogant; he is pleased to find that the infant has the physical disabilities of many of the classical worthies—Cicero's wart, Alexander's wry neck, Marius's tumorous legs, and one short leg like Agesilaus—all of which lead the father to hope that the boy will stutter like Demosthenes and enjoy the unfortunate defects of other great men (p. 100). He will not let the boy be swaddled; he scolds the midwife in a fine comic scene:

"Swaddle him! (quoth he) far be it from me to submit to such a pernicious Custom. Is not my son a Man? and is not Man the Lord of the Universe? Is it thus you use this Monarch at his first arrival in his dominions, to manacle and shackle him hand and foot? Is this what you call to be free-born? If you have no regard to his natural Liberty, at least have some to his natural Faculties." (p. 100)

Cornelius and the nurse wrangle on, but Mrs. Scriblerus breaks into the argument:

"My dear, I have had many disputes with you upon this subject before I was a month gone: We have but one child, and cannot afford to throw him away upon experiments. I'll have my boy bred up like other gentlemen, at home, and always under my own eye." (pp. 100 - 101)

Cornelius rises to one of his finest oratorical moments as he explodes and outlines the grandiose travels he has in mind for the education of the boy:

"What, bred at home? Have I taken all this pains for a creature that is to lead the inglorious life of a Cabbage, to suck the nutritious juices from the spot where he was first planted? No; to perambulate this terraqueous Globe is too small a Range; were it permitted, he should at least make the Tour of the whole System of the Sun." (p. 101)

Nothing will be too difficult for the young sage; rather than look at maps or listen to the lies of travelers, he will "make his own Legs his

Compasses" to measure the earth and the highest mountains and visit Ararat, Athos, and Olympus as well as the famous volcanoes (among them Etna and Vesuvius). He shall also study volcanic eruptions, earthquakes, thunder, and storms; he will survey the deserts of Arabia and Tartary. But this is too much for Mrs. Scriblerus, and she falls into hysterics, whereupon Cornelius is shoved out of the room by her women friends (p. 101).

Like the boyhood of Tristram Shandy in Sterne's novel, that of Martin is burdened by the theories of his father, and his education is perverted. In Chapter III his christening is marred by the fact that the maid has scoured the rust from the old shield used as his baptismal cradle (his father wanting him to be cradled in an ancient shield, like Hercules). Here the satire seems to be Arbuthnot's, for the episode of the shield seems to be a revival of his old feud with Dr. John Woodward (who later buys the shield), an antiquarian who was addicted to the purchase of classical artifcats and was to be pilloried several years later in Pope, Gay, and Arbuthnot's farce, *Three Hours after Marriage*.[13]

The education and nutrition of young Martinus are sources of constant disagreement among Cornelius, his wife, and the nurse. The nurse is not allowed to eat beef, for although it will make him physically strong, it will dull and clog his intellect. Diet, Cornelius believes, is a strong influence on intellectual growth, and the nurse leaves the family when the old pedant tries to force her to dine on the teats of a pregnant sow (pp. 105 - 107). Martin learns his catechism by means of a puppet show, and the rest of his education is similarly "practical": a geographical suit of clothes (French hat with an African feather, Dutch shirts, Flanders lace, Italian gloves, Spanish shoes, and some English clothing lined with silk from India), sign posts to teach him about animals, and fruits for instruction about foreign agriculture (p. 107). Even his mathematics is also learned at the table: "His disposition to the Mathematicks was discover'd very early, by his drawing parallel lines on his bread and butter, and intersecting them at equal Angles, so as to form the whole Superficies into squares" (pp. 107 - 108).

In languages he encounters some difficulties because he cannot for three months proceed to the letter D until he has mastered the pronunciation of C "in the ancient manner," and his mastery of writing is delayed because the writing teacher knows nothing of the waxen tables of Fabius. His father, determined that the boy proceed in the manner of Montaigne, insists that he learn and speak nothing

but the classical languages, particularly the Greek, in which he is
forced to eat and drink (as Homer was supposed to have done):

But what most conduced to his easy attainment of this Language, was his
love of Ginger-bread; which his Father observing, caused it to be stampt
with the Letters of the Greek Alphabet; and the child the very first day eat
as far as Iota. By his particular application to this language above the rest,
he attain'd so great a proficience therein, that Gronovius ingenuously confesses he durst not confer with this child in Greek at eight years old; and at
fourteen he composed a Tragedy in the same language, as the younger
Pliny had done before him. (p. 108)

He also learns the Arabic, Hebrew, Syrian and Chaldaic tongues,
and writes imitations of *The Arabian Nights* and the lamentably in-
competent translations of the *Persian Tales* by Ambrose Philips, the
Grub Street hack who was a favorite subject of the satirical comments and public animosity of Pope, Swift, Gay, and Henry Carey,
the latter giving Philips an undying fame as "Namby-Pamby."[14]

The satire on education continues in Chapters V, VI, and VII as
Martin's innocent childhood games are turned to pedagogical advantage by his father, who insists that only those games employed
by the ancients or their modern followers are worthy of the boy's
attention. Cornelius believes that

"*Play* was invented by the *Lydians* as a remedy against *Hunger*. Sophocles
says of Palamedes, that he invented *Dice* to serve sometimes instead of a
dinner. It is therefore wisely contrived by Nature, that Children, as they
have the keenest *Appetites*, are most addicted to *Plays*. From the same
cause, and from the unprejudic'd and incorrupt simplicity of their minds it
proceeds, that the Plays of the Ancient Children are preserv'd more entire
than any other of their Customs. In this matter I would recommend to all
who have any concern in my Son's Education, that they deviate not in the
least from the primitive and simple Antiquity." (p. 109)

These games are supposed to teach virtue and morality, but in ac-
cordance with his father's theory he also learns "an odd and secret
manner of Stealing, according to the Custom of the Lacedoem-
onians; wherein he succeeded so well, that he practised it to
the day of his death" (p. 111).

Disaster often follows in the wake of the theories of Cornelius. To
all of his wife's fears and protests, he simply answers, "Let a
Daughter be the care of her Mother, but the Education of a Son

should be the delight of his Father'' (p. 112). And so Martin learns gymnastics and breaks a leg; Cornelius tries to set it with a split reed and an ancient charm in the manner of Pliny and Cato, but relents to have it set by a physician when after five days it does not begin to heal (p. 112).

Martin also learns dancing, but only the tragic mode (the ancients, according to Cornelius, disliked the comic and the satiric). But the father (citing Pliny) also insists that Martin's spleen be removed so as to make him a better runner; Mrs. Scriblerus, again harried and horrified by her husband's rampant pedagogy, objects and pleads with her brother-in-law Albertus to intervene and prevent the operation. At this point Albertus emerges as a foil to his brother, for he is everything Cornelius is not: discreet, sober, unpedantic, and sensible. Occasionally successful in dissuading Cornelius from some of his wilder schemes, he argues against the removal of the spleen by suggesting that speed of foot is a cowardly trait shared by lechers (pp. 113 - 14).

In general Albertus tends, though favorably disposed toward the ancients, to argue a sensible position that modern learning, too, has its merits, but his mention of music-masters throws Cornelus into a passion against modern music, which he characterizes as "fiddling," and in favor of ancient music and its power to move the emotions. In one of the best farcical scenes in the book, Cornelius, trying to prove his charges against modern music, grabs his lyre to pacify two women apple-sellers:

With that Cornelius, undress'd as he was, jumps out into his Balcony, his Lyra in hand, in his slippers, with his breeches hanging down to his ankles, a stocking upon his head, and a waistcoat of murrey-colour'd sattin upon his body: He touch'd his Lyra with a very unusual sort of an Harpegiatura, nor were his hopes frustrated. The odd Equipage, the uncouth Instrument, the strangeness of the Man and of the Musick drew the ears and eyes of the whole Mob that were got about the two female Champions, and at last of the Combatants themselves. They all approach'd the Balcony, in as close attention as Orpheus's first Audience of Cattle, or that of an Italian Opera when some favourite Air is just awaken'd. This sudden effect of his Musick encouraged him mightily, and it was observ'd he never touch'd his Lyre in such a truly chromatick and enharmonick manner as upon that occasion. The mob laugh'd, sung, jump'd, danc'd, and us'd many odd gestures, all which he judg'd to be caused by his various strains and modulations. (p. 116)

But Cornelius fails to see his own foolishness and ends his recital "with the utmost Exultation in himself, and Contempt of his Brother; and, it is said, behav'd that night with such unusual haughtiness to his family, that they all had reason to wish for some ancient Tibicen [flute-player] to calm his Temper" (p. 117).

Having been disappointed in so many of his pedagogical schemes, Cornelius turns to Martin's education in rhetoric, logic, and metaphysics, and selects as his son's fellow student young Conradus Crambe, who is as much a pedant as his employer. The two lads are soon at their studies; Martin can grasp only material objects, but Crambe is deeply in love with mere words and symbols. They plunge into discussions of reality and appearance, metaphysics, universals. Most comic is Crambe's *Treatise of Syllogisms*, in which he

suppos'd that a Philosopher's brain was like a great Forest, where Ideas rang'd like animals of several kinds; that those Ideas copulated and engender'd Conclusions; that when those of different Species copulate, they bring forth monsters or absurdities; that the *Major* is the male, the *Minor* the female, which copulate by the Middle Term, and engender the Conclusion. Hence they are call'd the *praemissa*, or Predecessors of the Conclusion; and it is properly said by the Logicians *quod pariunt scientiam, opinionem*; they *beget* science, opinion, &c. Universal Propositions are Persons of quality; and therefore in Logick they are said to be of the first *Figure*: Singular Propositions are Private persons, and therefore plac'd in the third or last figure, or rank. From those Principles all the rules of Syllogisms naturally follow. (p. 121)

Proceeding to develop ten rules of logic, Crambe extends his sexual metaphor by describing various aspects of logic in terms of barrenness, prostitution, inheritance, congenital disease, divorce, separation, incest, and bastardy. Absurdity in logic is a monster, falsity a bastard, a *non sequitur* an adopted child, and enthymeme (an argument with an implied premise or conclusion) a secret marriage (p. 122).

The two students then practice their logic on a set of fourteen theses, among them such impressively ludicrous metaphysical questions as whether God loves a "possible" angel more than an existing fly, whether angels are more perceptive in the morning, whether females can be born innocent, or whether "the Creation was finish'd in six days, because six is the most perfect number, or if six be the most perfect number because the Creation was finish'd in six days" (pp. 123 - 24). In the episodes on logic, rhetoric, and metaphysics, the Scriblerians satirize and parody ancient, medieval, and Renaissance thinkers as diverse as Aristotle, Democritus, Descartes, Aquinas, Francisco Suarez, and Locke, who are ridiculed for their logic-chopping and pedantry. [15] This distrust of the intellectuals is typical of much Scriblerian writing, as, for example, in Book III of *Gulliver's Travels* or the well-known couplet in Pope's *Essay on Man*:

> Know then thyself, presume not God to scan;
> The proper study of Mankind is Man.

Crambe and Martin thus take their place among that sturdy band of pseudointellectuals to be found in eighteenth-century satire.

The satire moves on to anatomy in Chapter VIII. The anatomical studies of Martin and Crambe suffer a setback when they purchase the corpse of a criminal and set out to take it back to their laboratory "near the Pest-fields in St. Giles's" close by Tyburn, the site of so many executions. They have to smuggle the corpse into their lodgings in order to avoid the landlord. As Crambe tries to spirit the body upstairs, the corpse nearly falls from his arms, and in tightening his grip around it, he causes the body to break wind. Crambe, terrified, throws down the body and rushes to tell Martin, whose assurances cannot make him resume the task: "You may say what you please . . . no man alive ever broke wind more naturally; nay he seemed to be mightily relieved by it." By this time the whole household has been awakened, and we have another of the lively farcical scenes:

The maid shriek'd; the landlady cry'd out Thieves; but the Landlord, in his shirt as he was, taking a candle in one hand, and a drawn sword in the other, ventur'd out of the Room. The maid with only a single petticoat ran up stairs, but spurning at the dead body, fell upon it in a swoon. Now the landlord stood still and list'ned, then he look'd behind him, and ventur'd down in this manner one stair after another, till he came where lay his maid, as dead, upon another corps unknown. The wife ran into the street and cry'd out Murder! (p. 126)

Crambe and Martin are captured and carried off by the watch to a justice of the peace, who asks them their profession, to which Crambe replies with comically misleading accuracy: "It is our business to imbrue our hands in blood; we cut off the heads, and pull out the hearts of those that never injur'd us; we rip up big-belly'd women, and tear children limb from limb" (p. 127).

Martin desperately tries to set matters straight, but is not per-mitted to interrupt, while Crambe continues in a speech filled with puns on anatomy and violence which causes the justice to stare, the landlord and his wife to lift their eyes, and Martin to fret:

"May it please your Worship, as touching the body of this man, I can answer each head that my accusers alledge against me, to a hair. They have hitherto talk'd like num-sculls without brains; but if your Worship will not only give ear, but regard me with a favourable eye, I will not be brow-beaten by the supercilious looks of my adversaries, who now stand cheek by jowl by your Worship. I will prove to their faces, that their foul mouths have not open'd their lips without a falsity; though they have shew'd their teeth as if they would bite off my nose. Now, Sir, that I may fairly slip my neck out of the collar, I beg this matter may not be slightly skin'd over. Tho' I have no man here to back me, I will unbosom myself, since Truth is on my side, and shall give them their bellies full, though they think they have me upon the hip. Whereas they say I came into their lodgings, with arms, and murder'd this man without their Privity, I declare I had not the least finger in it; and since I am to stand upon my own legs, nothing of this matter shall be left till I set it upon a right foot. In the vein I am in, I can-not for my heart's blood and guts bear this usage: I shall not spare my lungs to defend my good name: I was ever reckon'd a good liver; and I think I have the bowels of compassion. I ask but justice, and from the crown of my head to the soal of my foot I shall ever acknowledge myself your Worship's humble Servant." (p. 127)

Martin, after their dismissal by the justice, tries to fire Crambe, but gives up and takes him back into his service after another barrage of puns from his friend, who claims that he orders his life by the dictionary:

"Every day I am under the dominion of a certain Word: But this day in particular I cannot be misled, for I am govern'd by one that rules all sexes, ages, conditions, nay all animals rational and irrational. Who is not govern'd by the word Led? Our Noblemen and Drunkards are pimp-led, Physicians and Pulses fee-led, their Patients and Oranges pil-led, a New-married Man and an Ass are bride-led, an old-married Man and a Pack-horse are sad-led; Cats and Dice are rat-led, Swine and Nobility are sty-led, a Coquet and a Tinder-box are spark-led, a Lover and a Blunderer are grove-led." (p. 128)

In these two passages the Scriblerians achieve not only an amusing satire upon both anatomy and rhetoric but also attack a kind of mind which confuses words with fact, appearance with reality, and rant with substance.

In a very brief Chapter IX of about 200 words, we see Martin as a critic able "to convert every Trifle into a serious thing, either in the way of Life, or in Learning" (p. 129). By means of gathering similarities in sounds, words, and syllables, he emends and corrects Virgil, Horace, and Terence, "concluding that, if the *most correct* Authors could be so served with any reputation to the Critick, the amendment and alteration *of all the rest* would easily follow; whereby a new, a vast, nay boundless Field of Glory would be open'd to the true and *absolute Critick*" (p. 129). To Martin is attributed a piece on Virgil, under the names of Richard Bentley and Francis Hare, later appended to Pope's *Dunciad* as *Virgilius Restauratus*, which we will examine in the next chapter, as well as *Mr. John Ginglicutt's Treatise,* another satire upon criticism.

Just why the Scriblerians gave such short shrift to criticism in the *Memoirs* is curious when we recall that two of them had already written extensively upon the foibles of critics, Swift in *The Battle of the Books* and *A Tale of a Tub*, Pope in *An Essay on Criticism*; both had also been roughly handled by a variety of critics from William Wotton and Richard Bentley to John Dennis. Perhaps several members of the group intended to return to this topic at a later time but were prevented from doing so by the dissolution and dispersal of the circle in 1714. Only Pope was to take up the cudgels against the critics again, most notably in the evolving versions of the *Dunciad*.

Martin goes on to apply himself to physiology and psychology, disciplines in which Arbuthnot was more familiar than were his colleagues, and thus he may have written or supplied most of the details for this section. The young pedant studies venereal disease, but tiring of practice and research on rotten bodies, he turns to an analysis of the passions, their natures, and their sources. He examines vices and virtues and finds their sources in the human anatomy. Arguing by analogy that since animals are habitually immoral because of their physical attributes (wings, web feet, beaks, fangs, and muscles), he concludes that the body and soul are interdependent ("if you deprive the Mind of the outward Instruments whereby she usually expresseth that Passion, you will in time abate the Passion itself; in like manner as Castration abates Lust"). Thus, since the soul expresses each passion by a certain muscle, and since all muscles grow bigger and stronger by exercise, the strength of an individual's passion may be measured by the size and strength of his muscles. These premises accepted, he finds that the vices and virtues of mankind are exhibited in such bodily motions as nodding, bowing, bending, and tossing the head, though he is at a loss to explain affectation and immoderate laughter (pp. 131 - 33). The Scriblerians are satirizing past and current theories, as Kerby-Miller has demonstrated in his notes.[16]

Thus far the first ten chapters of the *Memoirs* are largely episodic, moving rapidly and lightly from one satiric target to another, leaving many situations begging for fuller and more dramatic treatment. Cornelius, the father of Martin, suddenly drops out of sight at the beginning of Chapter VIII (on anatomy) and never reappears: Crambe leaves at the end of Chapter X. Each chapter seems to stand by itself, and there are few attempts at transition between the episodes. But such is to be expected of a work of composite authorship which was never brought to a polished completion.

IV   Satire on Love and Law

However, in the next five chapters (XI through XV) the authors change the pace by providing, in addition to the usual types of satire seen in the previous section, a case history of a young nobleman at court and the extended narrative of Martin's courtship of and marriage to the Siamese twins Lindamira and Indamora. The story of the young aristocrat serves to illustrate Martin's theory and treatment of mental aberrations.

The nobleman is discovered to have become affected in his speech and whimsical in his behavior; he has begun "to ask odd questions, talk in verse to himself, shut himself up from his friends, and accessible to none, but Flatterers, Poets, and Pickpockets; till his Relations and old Acquaintance judged him to be so far gone, as to be a fit Patient for the Doctor," who examines him and determines his affliction to be love (p. 134). Assured by others that there is no woman involved, Martin finally asserts that the cause must be self-love. Interrogation of the man's aunt reveals that he is constantly attended by a houseful of flatterers, writes letters to himself, talks and dreams continually about himself, ogles himself in the mirror, and is fascinated by such baubles as gold snuffboxes, tweezer cases, and a diamond ring, all the while losing his sense of humor (pp. 134 - 36).

Martin prescribes that the nobleman wear a bob-wig, shun flatterers (and, most of all, Frenchmen), travel in England and Holland, receive the advice of a friend regarding the extravagance, pride, and prodigality of his ego-mistress, and avoid the affectation and foppery which have caused his condition. And finally, "Let him marry himself, perhaps he may run to the next pond to get rid of himself, the Fate of most violent Self-Lovers" (p. 136).

The episode is brief, but it breaks the pattern of the previous chapters and provides a welcome change of pace. The object of the satire is conventional enough (compare, for example, Steele's story of the young gentleman who foolishly spends the rest of his life trying to find again a beautiful young lady whose face he has seen only once—in a passing coach window; *Tatler* No. 1, April 12, 1709). Affectation and foppery were staples of Restoration and early eighteenth-century satire, and the Scriblerians could not ignore such a tempting subject.

Chapter XII deals with Martin's attempts to discover the seat of the soul, which he finds in the pineal gland. After observing that "Calves and Philosophers, Tygers and Statesmen, Foxes and Sharpers, Peacocks and Fops, Cock-Sparrows and Coquets, Monkeys and Players, Courtiers and Spaniels, Moles and Misers" have pineals of the same shape, he receives a letter from the Society of Freethinkers at the Grecian Coffeehouse; they assert that the soul does not exist, a thesis which they demonstrate by a mechanistic explanation of thought-processes (pp. 137 - 42). The subjects of the satire appear to be the theories of Descartes, the various modes of new thinking in religion under a variety of popular names (deism, freethinking, for example), and, specifically, the controversy regarding the materiality of the soul which raged between the freethinker Anthony Collins and the metaphysician Samuel Clarke in the first decade of the century. [17]

In Chapters XIV and XV (the first edition does not contain a Chapter XIII) the satirists turn to a grotesque account of Martin in love. As Martin is walking near Whitehall, he meets a sideshow of assorted animals (leopard, porcupine, lion, cougar, baboon) and some unfortunate human beings—a black dwarf prince named Ebn-Hai-Paw-Waw and "two Bohemian Damsels whom Nature had as closely united as the ancient Hermaphroditus and Salmacis; and whom it was impossible to divide, as the mingled waters of the gentle Thames and the amorous Isis" (p. 143). He pays his sixpence and enters the sideshow, listens to the natural-history harangue of Mr. Randal, the keeper of the mysteries, and is completely enraptured by the twins: "Lindamira's eyes were of a lively blue; Indamora's were black and piercing. Lindamira's cheeks might rival the blush of the morning; in Indamora the Lilly overcame the Rose. Lindamira's tresses were of the paler Gold, while the Locks of Indamora were black and glossy as the Plumes of a Raven" (p. 146).

Martin falls in love with Lindamira, returns to his room in a love-lassitude, fruitlessly turns over Ovid's poems to find a sentiment compatible with his own, and writes his own apostrophe to the goddess of love. He first sighs and speaks of his love as "shame," then apologizes for doing so since the great worthies of literature and history have been moved by love. Were Lindamira some ordinary girl, "some gaudy Virgin," his love might be shameful to the heroes and gods; but his pleasure is doubled:

If there are charms in two eyes, two breasts, two arms; are they not all redoubled in the Object of my Passion? What tho' she be the common Gaze of the Multitude, and is follow'd about by the stupid and the ignorant; does she not herein resemble the greatest Princes, and the greatest Beauties? (p. 147)

After a second visit to the show, this time arousing the suspicion of Randal, he rushes home to write a love letter of the gushiest sort, so reminiscent of the *billet-doux* in the romantic fiction of the time:

To the most amiable LINDAMIRA

WHile others, O darling of Nature, look upon thee with the eyes of Curiosity, I behold thee with those of Love. Since I have been struck with thy most astonishing Charms, how have I call'd upon Nature to make a new head, new arms, and a new body to sprout from this single Trunk of mine, and to double every member, so as to render me a proper Mate for so lovely a Pair? but think to how little purpose it will be for thee to stay till Nature shall form another of thy kind! In such beauties she exhausts her whole art, and cannot afford to be prodigal. Ages must be numbred, nay perhaps some Comet may vitrify this Globe on which we tread, before we behold such a Castor and a Pollux resembling the beauteous Lindamira and Indamora. Nature forms her wonders for the Wise, and such a Master-piece she could design for none but a Philosopher. Cease then to display those beauties to the profane Vulgar, which were created to crown the desires of

Your Passionate Admirer,

MARTINUS SCRIBLERUS (p. 149)

The letter is intercepted by the villainous Randal, who arranges an assignation in a room adjoining Lindamira's; Martin arrives and is attacked by the cougar. Lindamira intervenes, and the cat turns upon her, "wounding three of her hands and her two noses," but Martin rescues her, and she falls in love with him (pp. 150 - 51).

But their bliss is marred by the emergence of a romantic triangle as the other twin, Indamora, also becomes enamored of the gallant Martin, and she wails at her misfortune:

Wretched Indamora! if Lindamira must never more see Martin, Martin shall never again bless the eyes of Indamora. Yet why do I say wretched, since my Rival can never possess my Lover without me? The pangs that others feel in Absence, from the thought of those Joys that bless their Rivals, can never sting thy bosom; nor can they mortify thee by making thee a Witness, without giving thee at the same time a share, of their Endearments. Change then thy proceeding, Indamora; thy Jealousy must act a new and unheard-of part, and promote the interest of thy Rival, as the only way to the enjoyment of thy Lover. (pp. 151 - 52)

Thus a lovelorn heroine takes her place in the tradition of the women who sacrifice their own interests for those of another woman, and the parody of the *Memoirs* is broadened to include that of the romance, a type of literature to which none of the Scriblerians was addicted and which they all would have despised.

Not only the literary romance is parodied in the persons of the grotesque twin heroines and their unlikely lover, but also perhaps something of the epic itself. As in the great epics the major antagonists must come to individual combat, so Martin must prove his mettle. When Martin manages to elope with Lindamira, she is attacked by the lecherous baboon (the "Manteger") as she climbs out the window. Martin moves to defend his bride, and the ensuing battle plays delightfully upon the traditional combats of the epic heroes:

Three times the hot Manteger, frighted at the furious menaces of his An-
tagonist, made a circle round the chamber, and three times the swift-footed
Martin pursued him. He caught up the *Horn* of a *Unicorn*, which lay ready
for the entertainment of the curious spectator, and brandishing it over his
head in airy circles, hurled it against the hairy son of Hanniman; who
wrinkling his brown forehead, and gnashing his teeth in indignation,
stoop'd low: The horny Lance just ras'd his left shoulder, and stuck into the
tapestry hangings. Provok'd at this, the grinning Offspring of Hanniman
caught up the pointed *Horn* of an *Antelope,* and aim'd a blow against his
undismay'd Adversary. (pp. 152 - 53)

While Lindamira, "like another Helen from the Trojan wall,"
watches with fear for the outcome and love for her hero, the two antagonists go at it manfully. Martin protects himself by using his hat
as a shield, which blunts the point of the antelope horn, and he suffers only a tear in his breeches. And then he hits the beast on the
jaw with the foot of an elk, whereupon the baboon

clamber'd up his back, and pluck'd up by the roots a mighty grasp of
hair—but Martin soon dismounted him, and kept him at a distance. Love
not only inspired his breast with Courage, but gave double strength to his
Sinews; he heav'd up the *hand* of a prodigious *Sea-Monster;* which when
the chatt'ring Champion beheld, he no less furious, wielded the pond'rous
Thigh-bone of a *Giant.* And now they stood opposed to each other like the
dread Captain of the seven-fold Shield and the redoubted Hector. The
Thigh-bone miss'd its aim; but the hand of the Sea-Monster descended
directly on the head of the Sylvan Ravisher. The Monster chatter'd horri-
ble; he stretch'd his quiv'ring limbs on the floor; and eternal sleep lock'd
fast his eyelids. (p. 153)

The loving couple-trio escapes and are married by a clergyman in
the Fleet, a prison for debtors.

Having paid their respects to the tradition of the epic in Martin's
battle amid the curiosities of Randal's sideshow, Martin and his
double-mistress are frustrated in their attempt to consummate the
marriage as Randal obtains a warrant and hails them into court.
Chapter XV deals at length with the legal tribulations of Martin and
in so doing provides us with some of the funniest and most pointed
satire on law in the early eighteenth century.[18] The charges brought
by Randal raise issues of involuntary servitude (on Indamora's part),
concubinage, rape, bigamy, and incest, the latter two being the for-
mal indictments brought against the unfortunate bridegroom. The

situation is further complicated by the fact that Randal has married the black dwarf prince to Indamora. Martin is represented at the trial before the ecclesiastical court by Dr. Penny-Feather and Randal by Dr. Leatherhead.

By means of ingenious legalistic quibbling and the citation of numerous precedents from Scripture, history, philosophy, and theology, Penny-Feather proves that Lindamira-Indamora, having only one sex organ between them, is one person, that they thus constitute one wife, and therefore that Ebn-Hai-Paw-Waw (the dwarf) has no legal right to separate Martin and Lindamira. Leatherhead, on the other hand, argues by similarly learned evidence that the two women are separate persons and that therefore Martin is guilty of either incest or bigamy—or both (pp. 156 - 62).

The verdict of the judge is equally ingenious and as ludicrous as the arguments of the barristers, but it pleases neither party, for its purported wisdom suggests that law sometimes satisfies neither justice nor humaneness:

GENTLEMEN:
I am of the opinion that Lindamira and Indamora are distinct persons, and that both the Marriages are good and valid: Therefore I order you, Martinus Scriblerus, Batchelor in Physick, and you, Ebn-Hai-Paw-Waw, Prince of Monomotapa, to co-habit with your wives, and to lie in bed each on the side of his own wife. I hope, Gentlemen, you will seriously consider, that you are under a stricter Tye than common Brothers-in-law; that being, as it were, joint Proprietors of one common Tenement, you will so behave as good fellow lodgers ought to do, and with great modesty each to his respective sister-in-law, abstaining from all farther Familiarities than what Conjugal Duties do naturally oblige you to. Consider also by how small Limits the Duty and the Trespass is divided, lest, while ye discharge the duty of Matrimony, ye heedlesly slide into the sin of Adultery. (pp. 162 - 63)

Martin's appeal to a higher court is denied, but the Commission of Delegates reverses the judgment and dissolves both marriages "as proceeding upon a natural, as well as legal Absurdity" (p. 163).

This double-mistress episode is the most fully developed section of the *Memoirs* and gives the work a touch of the dramatic which it for the most part otherwise lacks. It also provides a burlesque of the plots, characters, and devices of romantic fiction, as well as a parody of the precious and overwrought language of such writing. There are, furthermore, several devices of the mock-epic, as in the battle between Martin and the baboon. The authors of the *Memoirs*, as Kerby-Miller believes, overcame the problem of the variance of the literary style of this episode from that of the other parts of the book by attributing the piece to Martin himself, a storyteller far more literarily alive than the narrator, but the attempt is rather clumsy.[19] The episode is, furthermore, flawed by the *deus ex machina* of the Commission of Delegates which voids the judge's decision; thus the authors spared themselves the difficulty of either developing the implications of the amusing *ménage à quatre* or leaving the four as the victims of a hairsplitting judge and their own conflicting emotions. Despite its flaws, however, the story of Martin in love is one of the few instances in which the Scriblerians achieve some success in fusing character, plot, theme, and dialogue. Had the *Memoirs* been subjected to extensive revision and the discipline of one editor-writer, it might have better unity and balance.

The last two chapters of the *Memoirs* follow Martin in his travels as he tries to recover from his sorrow over his loss of Lindamira. Starting out in 1699, he takes four voyages: on the first, as a result of a storm, he discovers the "Remains of the ancient *Pygmaean* Empire"; on the second he goes to "the Land of the *Giants*, now the most humane people in the world"; on the third he visits "a whole Kingdom of *Philosophers*, who govern by the *Mathematicks*"; and on the final journey "he discovers a Vein of Melancholy proceeding almost to a disgust of his Species" (pp. 164 - 65). The club never got around to fleshing out these travels, though one minor writer attempted to do so about ten years after the publication of the *Memoirs*.[20] More interesting, however, is the strong likelihood that Swift, a few years later, drew upon this material for the four voyages of *Gulliver's Travels*, in which the journeys of the hero to various lands follow in succession and subject matter the itinerary of Chapter XVI of the *Memoirs*.

The concluding chapter (XVII) lists "*the Discoveries and Works of the Great* Scriblerus, *made and to be made, written and to be written, known and unknown,*" among them discoveries in mathematics, physics, astronomy, mechanics, hydraulics, philosophy, demography, politics, poetry, medicine, and architecture (pp. 166 - 69), all of which lead the narrator to call him "this excellent Person, this Prodigy of our Age; who may well be called *The Philosopher of Ultimate Causes*, since by a Sagacity peculiar to himself, he hath discover'd Effects in their very Cause; and without the trivial helps of Experiments, or Observations, hath been the

Inventor of most of the modern Systems and Hypotheses" (p. 166). Appended to the *Memoirs* is a list of Martin's works, both published and unpublished. And with this parting shot at modern learning, its arrogance, its ignorance, and its pedantry, the Scriblerians put down their pens and dispersed, each to his own projects.

V   *The Eternal Pedant*

Although the *Memoirs* has never achieved the fame of many of the other works of its authors, it is important as a reflection of early eighteenth-century attitudes toward literature and learning. Of the members of the circle, Swift (*The Battle of the Books* and *A Tale of a Tub*, both 1704), Pope (the first version of *The Rape of the Lock*, 1712), and Arbuthnot (*The Art of Political Lying* and the *John Bull* pamphlets) had published major satires before the founding of the club and the beginning of work on the *Memoirs;* within a year Gay was to join their ranks with the publication of the mock-pastoral *Shepherd's Week.* In the years to follow, each was to become more involved with the kind of satire found in the adventures of Martinus Scriblerus. And, ironically, Pope, Swift, Gay, and Arbuthnot were to see themselves pilloried in a play by Colley Cibber in 1721.[21]

The age was particularly appropriate for satire on learning as science, increasingly free from the chains of classical and medieval authority as well as other technical and intellectual restrictions, and increasingly accepted in ever-widening circles, began to develop the foundations from which important discoveries were to be made and to point the way to what seemed to be the potential for unlimited human progress.[22] As the impact of the new science was made manifest in the work of Sir Issac Newton, William Harvey, Edmund Halley, Sir Robert Boyle, and a host of others, as the interest in antiquities began to flourish in the Restoration, and as the old pseudosciences (astrology and alchemy, for example) began to wither, an extravagant faith in man's ability for improving his own material and moral condition began to spread throughout western Europe. Somehow, it seemed, there was nothing which man could not attain if only he applied himself diligently and rationally to his problems. But, as in every age, there were those who questioned the validity of the premises and conclusions of the modernists.

Thus in *The Memoirs of Martinus Scriblerus* we find the authors attacking what they conceive to be false learning in medicine, psychology, law, criticism, theology, literature, and education. Martin, his father Cornelius, and Crambe are stereotypes of the virtuoso-pedant who is unable to distinguish between the trivial and the important, the appearance of learning and true wisdom, true and false knowledge. The three are arrogantly proud of their intellectuality, obstinate in their insistence upon the rightness of their learned pursuits, and totally impotent in advancing the cause of true learning as they push on through adventures which, like those of Voltaire's Candide, should expose the foolishness of their theorizing. For the Scriblerians these dolts are symptomatic of a world in which the old values, common sense, and man's knowledge of his own limitations have become inverted, indeed perverted. The book is permeated with much of the anti-intellectualism found in both Swift and Pope, a dark suspicion of the Bentleys, the Wottons, the Dennises, and the contributors to the *Philosophical Transactions*.

As an attack on pedantry the *Memoirs* is frequently amusing, but it is only modestly successful in the whole, as works of composite authorship often are when they lack the firm control of a guiding hand to order the ideas and fashion the disparate pieces into a polished, fluent, and coherent work of art. Just what directions the Scriblerians might have taken in their joint efforts are impossible to know. But as it stands the *Memoirs* often suffers from a failure to develop potentially dramatic situations; the biographical framework is certainly adequate, but the rich supportive details are lacking. There are some occasionally brisk passages of dialogue, and there are a number of fine farcical scenes worthy of Henry Fielding, Tobias Smollett, or Laurence Sterne. Though incomplete and in some ways unsatisfactory, *The Memoirs of Martinus Scriblerus* remains a readable and engaging comment upon the intellectual world of early eighteenth-century England.

CHAPTER 5

Other Satires on Learning

F ROM the dispersal of the members of the Scriblerus circle in 1714 until his death, Arbuthnot occasionally continued the attack on pedantry, though much of his later writing was devoted to more scholarly topics. During the years from 1714 through 1732 he wrote three more satires on false learning and collaborated on another: *Three Hours after Marriage*, a moderately successful farce written in partnership with Gay and Pope (produced in 1717), *Virgilius Restauratus*, a parody of philological criticism printed in 1729, *A Brief Account of Mr. John Ginglicutt's Treatise*, a satire upon the language of political argument published in 1731, and *An Essay Concerning the Origin of the Sciences*, a continuation of the Scriblerian attack on learning which appeared in 1732.

All of these satires are connected in one way or another with the satire and parody which emerged in Arbuthnot's political satires of 1712 or in the work of the Scriblerians in 1713 - 1714. Two of them—the essay on the sciences and the parody of Virgilian scholarship—are related to the fictional career of Martinus Scriblerus, while John Ginglicutt's treatise parallels the subject matter of *The Art of Political Lying*. *Three Hours after Marriage* is less obviously tied to the Scriblerian or political materials, but it, too, ridicules modern pedantry. Each work has some amusing patches, but none rises to the level of the *Memoirs*, and none shows the sustained vitality of *The History of John Bull*.

I   Three Hours after Marriage

After his first work with the Scriblerus group, Arbuthnot's next venture into satire on learning appeared on Wednesday, January 16, 1717, when *Three Hours after Marriage*, a comedy written in collaboration with Pope and Gay, was first produced at the theater in Drury Lane. The play ran for seven nights and was moderately successful, though some modern critics are disposed to think it rather mediocre.[1] Pope and Arbuthnot had had no practical experience with the stage, and the controversy which swirled about the play after its first production probably discouraged both writers from ever again venturing to write for the theater. Gay, however, had written three plays before joining forces with Pope and Arbuthnot—*The Mohocks* (1712), *The Wife of Bath* (1713), and *The What D'ye Call It* (1715), none of them successful (*The Mohocks*, in fact, was not produced)—and his must have been the guiding spirit in the joint effort. Undiscouraged by his lack of success, he was to go on to write the most famous ballad-opera of the century, *The Beggar's Opera* (1728).

The plot of the play is simple, episodic, and farcical. Dr. Fossile, an antiquarian and pedant over sixty years old, brings home his bride, Mrs. Townley, a worldly-wise young woman of twenty-three, but within minutes he discovers himself a potential cuckold at the hands of two more virile and ingenious young rivals, Plotwell and Underplot, who assume various disguises (including those of a Polish doctor, a patient, a mummy, and a crocodile) to regain access to their former lover. The action consists of Plotwell and Underplot's strategems to get at the young wife, her attempts to conceal from Fossile her lubricious past and her previous relationship with the young rakes, and Fossile's feverish attempts to foil them, all of this business complicated by the desire of Fossile's niece, Phoebe Clinket, to get her play produced, and by the appearance and learned discussions of two other doctors, Possum and Nautilus, and the apothecary Ptisan. Fossile is frustrated at the end of the play by the revelation that Mrs. Townley is already married to Lieutenant Bengall, just returned from the West Indies after three years' absence, and his agony is compounded when she gives him her infant bastard.

The play is conventional farce in almost every way, relying upon such appropriately tag-named stock characters as the pedant with an obsession for collecting weird artifacts and absurd theories (Fossile), the wife whose chaste exterior masks a lascivious heart (Mrs. Townley, who unlike Margery Pinchwife in William Wycherley's *Country Wife* knows the city and its temptations all too expertly), a dilettante poetess of minimal talent and maximum conceit (Phoebe Clinket, whose maid moves about with a writing table on her back and whose name suggests the preciousness and jingling hollowness of her writing), a foreigner who speaks ludicrous English (Dr. Lubomirski, a Pole who is actually Plotwell in disguise), a maid who tries to abet and conceal her mistress's liaisons (Sarsnet, suggesting softness and silkiness), a sailor (Jack Capstone), an apothecary (Ptisan, suggesting a patent medicine), and the lively rakes (Plotwell and Underplot). To the audience at Drury Lane, these were characters whose stage ancestors in the English drama of the past century and a half were easily recognizable.

Nor are the plot devices any more original in either their conception or use. The play is filled with concealed, forged, and discovered letters; overheard conversations; hasty concealments to avoid embarrassing discoveries; compromising situations; readings of absurd poetry; climactic discoveries with surprising consequences and reversals; sudden retreats. Despite their long stage history they come together with the stock characters to provide a lively farce and to demonstrate the old truism that what seems conventional (and thus dull) to the literary critic and historian may be rather funny to the audience.

The seven-night run of the play (hardly a short one by early eighteenth-century standards) may perhaps also be accounted for by the pointed personal satire in the persons of Fossile, Phoebe Clinket, Sir Tremendous, and Plotwell. Fossile is undoubtedly Arbuthnot's old whipping-boy, Dr. Woodward, though not all aspects of the pedant's character are drawn from him.[2] He is ignorant, proud, insensitive, bad-humored; he cares only for monsters and cannot command the Latin grammar of which he pretends to be a master. Phoebe Clinket has been linked to various female contemporaries, including the Countess of Winchilsea (unlikely because she was a friend of Pope and apparently was not bothered by the play), and Margaret, Duchess of Newcastle; but Susannah Centlivre (1667? - 1723), a notorious actress, the wife of a royal cook, and the author of eighteen plays, seems a more likely candidate.[3] Clinket is an unsuccessful playwright who cannot get her plays produced, and she confesses to having five illegitimate children (which are, in fact, her unstaged plays). Sir Tremendous can be none other than John Dennis, the blustering old critic and himself a frustrated dramatist, a cantankerous literary man at whom several Augustan writers, particularly Pope (see, for example, *An Essay on Criticism*, lines 582 - 87—the famous "Appius" portrait), frequently aimed their ridicule.[4] And Plotwell, lover and man of the theater, may be Colley Cibber, the affable libertine and successful comic actor (especially as the fop), playwright, and theater-manager who played the role on opening night, and who, like Dennis, was the butt of much satire, most notably as the King of Dullness in Pope's final version of the *Dunciad*.[5]

Other elements besides the farce and the personal satire probably appealed to the audience at Drury Lane. Phoebe's difficulties with Plotwell and Sir Tremendous over the production of her play, the slapstick of the mummy and the crocodile, the frequent sexual innuendoes, and Act III's legal quibbling are still amusing. The dialogue, too, is often sprightly, especially when it is a vehicle for a parody of dramatic criticism as Sir Tremendous and Clinket exercise their wit on what they think is ancient plagiarism and modern incompetence:

Sir *Tremendous*. O what Felony from the Ancients! What Petty-Larceny from the Moderns! There is the famous *Iphigenia* of *Racine*, he stole his *Agamemnon* from *Seneca*, who stole it from *Euripides*, who stole it from *Homer*, who stole it from all the Ancients before him. In short there is nothing so execrable as our most taking Tragedys.
1st Player. O! but the immortal *Shakespear*, Sir.
Sir *Tremendous*. He had no Judgment.
2d Player. The famous *Ben. Johnson!*
Clinket. Dry.
1st Player. The tender *Otway!*
Sir *Tremendous*. Incorrect.
2d Player. *Etheridge!*
Clinket. Meer Chit-chat.
1st Player. *Dryden!*
Sir *Tremendous*. Nothing but a Knack of Versifying.
Clinket. Ah! dear Sir *Tremendous*, there is that *Delicatesse* in your Sentiments!
Sir *Tremendous*. Ah Madam! there is that Justness in your Notions![6]

And their dramatic criticism rapidly degenerates into *double-entendre:*

Clinket. I am so charm'd with your manly Penetration!
Sir *Tremendous*. I with your profound Capacity!
Clinket. That I am not able—
Sir *Tremendous*. That it is impossible—
Clinket. To conceive—
Sir *Tremendous*. To express—

Clinket. With what Delight I embrace —
Sir Tremendous. With what Pleasure I enter into—
Clinket. Your Ideas, most learned Sir *Tremendous!*[7]

Thus, as one editor has suggested, the play becomes "a comedy of humours—of literary delettantism, of obsessive antiquarianism and of sexual possessiveness."[8] Even modern audiences, at Oxford in 1953 and at Lake Erie College in 1960,[9] have found it attractive.

Whatever its merits as literature and as satire of modern learning and literature, the play became a center of controversy after its first performance. Within a week the first of a number of attacks appeared, and in late March John Brevall, behind the pseudonym of "Joseph Gay," published a play, *The Confederates,* which smartly pilloried the three authors, while Dennis and Cibber were also getting their revenge.[10]

As with *The Memoirs of Martinus Scriblerus,* the task of attributing specific passages to each of the three authors is difficult. Lester Beattie points out that it is conventional to assume that Fossile is the creation of Arbuthnot and that the medical and pharmaceutical allusions are his, but concludes that it "is hazardous to charge every powder-and-potion item to Arbuthnot. More important, even if he coined them, they are so intricately woven in with the general satire that only the shaping hand of an experienced dramatist can have made use of them," an opinion shared by G. A. Aitken.[11]

Three Hours after Marriage is an interesting but slight interlude in Arbuthnot's career, an entertaining play in an age which produced so little of lasting merit in the theater.

II   Virgilius Restauratus

Arbuthnot's next contribution to the continuing (though more and more sporadic) war against the pedants and their corrupt learning appeared in the variorum edition of Pope's *Dunciad* in 1729. The butt of ridicule in this short piece is the only enemy of the Scriblerians, Dr. Richard Bentley, now in his late sixties, who had been attacked by Swift in *The Battle of the Books* and *A Tale of a Tub* and by Pope in the earlier version of *The Dunciad* (1728). Bentley, without doubt England's greatest classical scholar in the eighteenth century, had by now been the subject of satirical attacks for over thirty years; his immense learning, his arrogance, and his corpulence evoked both envy and mirth. The wits, unable to challenge his learning, chose instead to fight him with their own weapons. Swift, for example, never forgave him for his aspersions on Sir William Temple in his "Dissertation upon the Epistles of Phalaris," appended to the second edition of William Wotton's *Reflections upon Ancient and Modern Learning* (1697), and proceeded to fix him firmly in literary history with the portrait of a garrulous, foul-mouthed, jealous braaggart in *The Battle of the Books*.[12]

Virgilius Restauratus is a parody of Bentley's methods of emending classical texts, as demonstrated in his editions of Horace (1711) and Terence (with the fables of Phaedrus, 1726). But Arbuthnot's title also recalls Lewis Theobald's *Shakespeare Restored* (1726), in which the lawyer-scholar attacked Pope's freewheeling editorial methods in his edition of Shakespeare in the previous year, for which Theobald was repaid with literary immortality as Cibber's predecessor as King of Dullness in the earlier versions of *The Dunciad*. In Arbuthnot's short parody, Bentley is represented as making about thirty textual changes in Book I of the *Aeneid* (verses 1, 52, 86, 117, 119, 122, 151, 154, 170, 188, 631, and 748) and Book II (verses 1, 3, 4, 5, 7, 9, and 13).[13]

Bentley is personified as Martinus Scriblerus, whose emendations are arrogant, pedantic, and precious. Insensitive to the genius and the free creative spirit of Virgil, and blind to the advantages of literary license, he emends without taste and in so doing appears ludicrously literal and petty. To detail all of these emendations would be tedious, but several examples will suffice to demonstrate the point of the satire. In Book I, verse 86, Virgil describes Aeolus as striking a mountain from which the winds escape "velut agmine facto" (like a column of troops), for which Martin, in the supposed manner of Bentley, substitutes "velut aggero fracto" (as when a dike breaks). And in Book I, verse 122, Martin finds incredible Virgil's description of "arma virum" (armor) afloat in the ocean and emends it to "armi hominum" (shoulders, upper arms) instead.[14] These and other emendations ridicule the pedantry and incompetence of critics who like "The True Critick" in Swift's *Tale of a Tub* is "*a Discoverer and Collector of Writers Faults*" and has the "Talent of swarming about the noblest Writers" in the manner of a rat near a cheese or a dog at a bone.[15] Or they recall Tom Folio in Addison and Steele's *Tatler* (Number 158, Thursday, April 13, 1710), the blockhead who damns Virgil because a modern editor has incorrectly punctuated two passages.

Arbuthnot's short parody is an extension of the suggestions of Martin's critical abilities given in Chapter IX of *The Memoirs of Martinus Scriblerus*, where we are told that the dullard's talents will be shown in his "Addenda to his Notes on the Dunciad."[16] Brief as it is, *Virgilius Restauratus* reflects the continuing Scriblerian distrust of modern learning and Arbuthnot's own amusement at the follies of the type of mind represented by Richard Bentley.

III   A Brief Account of Mr. John Ginglicutt's Treatise

Several years after the publication of the parody of Virgilian scholarship, Arbuthnot continued the satire on learning with *A Brief Account of Mr. John Ginglicutt's Treatise concerning the Altercation or Scolding of the Ancients* (1731). This, like *The Art of Political Lying*, purports to be a prospectus of the contents of a proposed book along with information concerning price and subscription: *"The price of the book in sheets is ten shillings, one half to be paid down; only the polemical writers on each side shall have one copy gratis; and my cousin Ginglicutt have two. Receipts will be delivered at Mr. Franklin's, Mr. Roberts's, Mr. Warner's, Mr. Peele's, and at most of the book and pamphlet-sellers in London and Westminister."*[17]

The *persona*, John Ginglicutt, emerges as a rather proud and arrogant intellectual given to pomposity and inflated language as he boasts of his humble origins (the son of a widowed London fishwife) and his liberal education ("I became thoroughly acquainted with the Greek and Roman authors"). He pompously announces that he seeks to "do something towards the honour of the place of my nativity, and to vindicate the rhetoric of this ancient forum of our metropolis from the aspersions of the illiterate" by composing the present treatise, in which, he claims solemnly, "I have demonstrated that the purity, sincerity, and simplicity of their diction is no where so well preserved as amongst my neighbourhood" (p. 382). With all of the self-assurance of a modern (who is, of course, correcting the mistakes of his less-enlightened colleagues), he, like a good rhetorician, lays out his major points: he will prove mistaken the notion that there is anything wrong with the sharpness and bitterness of present political argument; he will assuage the emotional wounds of those who think themselves damaged in such debates by showing that "calling of names is a true Greek and Roman eloquence"; he will show that English liberty will never be in danger so "long as this truly ancient and polite rhetoric subsists, which is both the symptom and cause of public liberty"; and he will provide advice and encouragement to "the promising geniuses which are daily rising in my native country" (pp. 382 - 83).

Having assured us of his competence and his good intentions, as well as his concern for the public welfare, Ginglicutt proceeds to analyze the nature of political name-calling. We must distinguish, he says, between "propriety and truth of speech," propriety being "when an author maketh use of the expression which is most apposite to his own idea, but doth not suppose the idea to be either absolutely true or false." Thus, in his first chapter, he claims that he will first

settle the original right of this sort of altercation, which is most indefeasible and unlimited in the female sex amongst all ranks and degrees except between old and young women; the latter being supposed to want the protection and benevolent assistance of the former. Secondly, that there is no mutual right of altercation between different sexes, except in the matrimonial state. Thirdly, that the right of altercation subsists between personages of equal rank, gods, goddesses, monarchs, generals, and public orators; likewise between republican orators and monarchs. Fourthly, between the people of free governments and their magistrates; but not between monarchs and their individual subjects. (p. 384)

With these generalizations established, he moves on to his proofs.

In the next thirteen paragraphs he establishes classical and historical precedents for name-calling by citing Olympian quarrels among Juno, Jupiter, and Venus (with, "for the benefit of the ladies, . . . a collection of epithets in use amongst the divinities, proper on parallel occasions; for sure no person of quality can think himself abused in the language of the goddesses?"), between Achilles and Agamemnon, Hector and Paris, Ulysses and Agamemnon, Philip of Macedon and Damades, Charles the Fifth and Francis the First, and others, to prove his point (pp. 384 - 89). He shows that epithets such as *insufferable, surly, bastard, fool, sot, usurper, cheat, parasite, prostitute, robber, rascal, mountebank, harlequin, pantomime, madman, hangman, temple-robber*, or their classical equivalents are common enough in quarrels among men and gods, even though "there is no reconciling most of this sort of altercation, nor the anger from which it proceeds, with the Christian morals; yet many Presbyters, Bishops, Popes, and some recorded as saints, have naturally fallen into it" (pp. 389 - 90).

This portion of the satire is perhaps the liveliest, for it shows us that little has changed in political debate over the centuries. The free and loose employment of terms such as *racist, liberal, radical, conservative, communist, socialist, reactionary, big-spender, law-and-order man,* and others by the politically ambitious who employ name-calling and demagoguery to hide questionable motives is still a part of our experience. Arbuthnot, having lived through the divisiveness created by the War of the Spanish Succession and the scandal of the South Sea Bubble, and having been associated with some writers, particularly Swift, who had used the same kinds of name-calling, knew well the appeal of such techniques.

Ginglicutt says that his next chapter will show how such altercations are useful and necessary to permit people to work off their frustrations in a manner harmless to the state, especially if such name-calling is confined to December and the Christmas season. Furthermore, such language will pose no real harm to the government or its officials, for this "altercation contributes exceedingly to the vigour of the administration, like the je-ho to loitering horses, that lug along the wheels of government" (pp. 390 - 91). The prospectus then tails off into matters of price, subscription, and publication.

Occasionally amusing and showing glints of Arbuthnot's best wit, the treatise fails to match the brilliance of his earlier satires. It would have benefited greatly from revision and polishing, but Arbuthnot, now in the last five years of his life and suffering increasingly from bad health, devoted no further attention to it. The work, consequently, reflects a consistent habit—to write a satire quickly and let it go on its way with little regard for either his own reputation or the improvement of the piece.

In this instance, as in most reactions to Arbuthnot's work, critical opinion, even among his contemporaries, was mixed. One of his friends, William Pulteney, Lord Bath, wrote to Swift on February 9, 1731:

If any of our Pamphletts (with which we abound) are ever sent over to Ireland, and you think them worth reading, you will perceive how low they are reduced in point of argument on one side of the Question. This has drove certain People to that resort of calling Names: *Villain Traytor Seditious Rascal* and such ingenious appellations have frequently been bestow'd on a couple of Friends of yours. Such usage has made it necessary to return the same polite language, and there has been more Billingsgate stuff utter'd from the Press within these two months than ever was known before. [18]

And after summarizing the contents of Arbuthnot's latest work, he states his own admiration: "His Quotations from Homer Demosthenes AEschines and Tully are admirable, & the whole is very humorously conducted."[19]

But Pope, writing to Swift on December 1 of the same year, was much less enthusiastic: "The paper you ask me about is of little value. It might have been a seasonable satire upon the scandalous language and passion with which men of condition have stooped to treat one another: surely they sacrifice too much to the people, when they sacrifice their own characters, families &c. to the diversion of that rabble of readers."[20] Pope's judgment is right; the few sparks of wit in the treatise seem forced and are not sufficient to redeem the piece and place it among Arbuthnot's better works. The mixed satire on learning and political language lacks the focus and zest of the earlier satires; it seems the work of a tired and ailing man.

IV   An Essay . . . Concerning the Origin of the Sciences

Arbuthnot's final satiric effort was a continuation of the Scriblerian activity in *An Essay of the Learned Martinus Scriblerus Concerning the Origin of the Sciences, Written to the Most Learned Dr. ———, F.R.S., from the Deserts of Nubia*, published in the third volume of the *Miscellanies* of Swift and Pope (1732). This piece, like many of the Scriblerian works, is probably of composite authorship, with Pope, Arbuthnot, and Parnell as contributors, and Arbuthnot's share, as Beattie suggests, probably being large.[21] The satire is again pointed at Dr. John Woodward, the battle-scarred opponent of many of the Scriblerians' wars, but by this time the ridicule touched upon the borders of the morbid: Woodward had died in 1728. Pope later told Spence that the purpose of the essay was "to ridicule such as build general assertions upon two or three loose quotations from the ancients."[22]

Writing from the "deserts" of Ethiopia, the learned Martin begins by asserting that "among all the inquiries which have been pursued by the curious and the inquisitive, there is none more worthy search of a learned head than the source from whence we derive those arts and sciences which raise us so far above the vulgar, the countries in which they rose, and the channels by which they have been conveyed."[23] The pedant dogmatically claims that all learning came to western Europe from Egypt and India, but says that the more remote sources are unknown. Troy and Thebes, he believes, were not the first empires; instead there was an earlier race called the Pygmaeans, whose existence he has discovered in random allusions in Homer, Aristotle, and other ancient writers. This tiny race, he assumes, also excelled in the arts of government, but eventually its survivors "retired into the depths of their deserts, where they lived undisturbed, till they were found out by Osiris in his travels to instruct mankind" (p. 361).

Martin then moves to prove his case by ambiguous references found in Diodorus Siculus, the first-century B.C. Greek historian, to "a sort of little Satyrs, who were hairy one half of their body, and whose leader Pan accompanied him in his expedition for the civilizing of mankind"; in Plutarch, who says that "they ate what they could get in the fields, their drink was water, and their bed was made of leaves or moss"; and in Herodotus, who tells us that they thought it a great feat to kill ants and creeping things. On the basis of this evidence Martin concludes that Egypt and India, both abounding in many simian species and both indulging in some sort of monkey-worship, reflect the sources of their knowledge (p. 362).

Turning to Greece, Martin demonstrates to his own satisfaction that Orpheus returned from Egypt and brought with him the term *satyrs* and the name of their leader, Pan. Citing Planudes, a medieval Byzantine grammarian and theologian, he asserts that the ancient fabulist Aesop himself was a descendant of that race, because the name Aesop, according to Planudes, may be a derivative of *Aethiope;* that Aesop was short, savage, and deformed; that he preferred living in the woods but deferred to society and came to court in his clothes; and that his satirical wit, his knowledge of animal nature, and his ability to speak with the beasts—all exhibited in the fables attributed to him—prove his origins (p. 363).

The remainder of Martin's proof is of much the same chop-logic, short-circuited nature. He cites Socrates as an example of an ancient with simian features, and suggests that some of the ancients cohabited with beasts: "This by degrees occasioned the hair of their posterity to grow higher than their middles: it arose in one generation to their arms, in the second it invaded their necks, in the ascendant of their heads, till the degenerate appearance, in which the species is now immersed, became completed" (p. 364). Similarly, in Italy, the Fauns found in Livy's history eventually became silent. Martin proceeds to evidence purportedly drawn from the reigns of Augustus and Constantine and from two monarchs of India—Perimal and Hanimant—to clinch his argument. But even though these ancient sages have sunk into bestiality and the dust of history, they still serve the cause of learning:

Yet, even at this time, what experiments do they not afford us, by relieving some from the spleen, and others from imposthumes, by occasioning laughter at proper seasons? with what readiness do they enter into the imitation of whatever is remarkable in human life? and what surprising relations have LeComte and others given of their appetites, actions, conceptions, affections, varieties of imaginations, and abilities of pursuing them? (p. 366)

These creatures have much to offer the world, and Martin thinks it shameful that such progenitors of learning should be treated so grossly in modern times (p. 366).

Proud and arrogant, he suggests that perhaps some apes in remote areas of the world may still possess the faculty of human speech and that scientists might still learn much from them by recovering past knowledge and advancing human wisdom. He pleads for the modern nations to accept them and for the whores, "the women with easy freedoms, and the gentlest treatment," to "oblige the loving creatures to sensible returns of humanity" (p. 367). But he regrets that that nation will not be Great Britain, because of its violent political factions, nor will it be Holland. With a nationalistic jab that must have pleased the Francophobes among his readers, Martin suggests that the only people capable of working compatibly with the apes are the French and the Jesuits (pp. 367 - 68).

The purpose of this satire, as Pope said, "was to ridicule such as build general assertions upon two or three loose quotations from the ancients." The point of the dedication to Dr. Woodward is ambiguous, except that it may refer obliquely to his *Remarks upon the Ancient and Present State of London* (1713), in which he had drawn various conclusions on the basis of archaeological evidence such as coins and urns. But more generally this Scriblerian essay makes fun of the kind of scholar in all ages who makes sweeping and sophomoric conclusions on scanty and misinterpreted evidence ripped from context and fitted into a procrustean argument. The thrust of the satire is not against scholarship and learning *per se*, but against pedantry, ignorance, and arrogance. Thus it takes its place among the other Scriblerian writings as well as Swift's *Tale of a Tub* and Book III of *Gulliver's Travels* and Pope's *Dunciad*.

V   *The Scourge of Pedantry*

In the four works examined in this chapter, several of them written in collaboration with other members of the Scriblerus group, Arbuthnot continued the attack on corruptions in learning and language which he had begun with *The Art of Political Lying* in 1712. Each employs techniques common to the satire of the Augustan period; the scholar, scientist, and critic as fool is a type character found in, among many others, Thomas Shadwell's Sir Nicholas Gimcrack (*The Virtuoso*, 1676), Samuel Johnson's Dick Minim (*The Idler*, 1759), and Richard Brinsley Sheridan's Sir Fretful Plagiary (*The Critic*, 1779). Even so, each of these four pieces is of interest to Arbuthnot's readers as a further and more revealing reflection of the mind of a lively and engaging writer who was also a reputable scientist in his own time, a man who could look at his own intellectual world with a high degree of comic detachment and then scourge the fools who brought discredit upon it.

CHAPTER 6

"A Great Philosopher"

A MONG his friends and contemporaries Arbuthnot was known not only as a talented and convivial satirist but also as an intellectual whose omnivorous curiosity and professional interests led him down paths hardly trod by Swift, Gay, or Pope, his close friends who knew just enough about science to make it a frequent subject of their attacks and a symbol of the decay of modern culture. Over a period of four decades, Arbuthnot wrote some eight scientific works, beginning with *Of the Laws of Chance* (1692) and continuing through *An Essay Concerning the Effects of Air on Human Bodies* (1733), which reflect his own diverse interests and those of his time in such areas as probability, geology, mathematics, metrics, numismatics, physiology, and dietetics. These works, the subject of this chapter, are not those which have earned him his place in literary history, and none has survived as a contribution to the advancement of learning. George Berkeley, his friend, could speak of him as "a great philosopher . . . reckoned the first mathematician of the age,"[1] but such a judgment had its source in friendship rather than scholarly assessment.

Writing as he was when experimental science had been largely freed from the shackles of classical authority by the work of Sir Francis Bacon, Sir William Harvey, Sir Isaac Newton, and others in the seventeenth century, and when the various scientific disciplines were beginning to bear fruit in a new technology, Arbuthnot moved easily in the community of medical men and experimenters, enjoying close friendships with men like Newton, Sir Hans Sloane, Dr. David Gregory, Dr. Richard Mead, and Dr. John Freind. Indeed, it is likely that his friendships and acquaintances among these people were more numerous than those among the literati. Certain it is that his interest in science was lifelong and did not diminish after his entrance into the fashionable world of the court and the company of the Scriblerian wits.

But, as in so much of his other writing, Arbuthnot's scientific work seems to suffer from the same indifference to his reputation that perhaps prevented him from becoming one of the major writers of the period. He was content to send a book into the world and then move on to other projects. Only one of his scientific works was revised, the one dealing with ancient coins, weights, and measures. A reading of these works reveals a lively and alert mind closely tuned to the scientific interests of the age. Most of the topics he takes up were ones that attracted the attention of his professional colleagues, and Arbuthnot moves through his materials with grace and intelligence.

This chapter will survey Arbuthnot's writings on science, beginning with *Of the Laws of Chance* (1692), through *An Examination of Dr. Woodward's Account of the Deluge* (1697), *An Essay on the Usefulness of Mathematical Learning* (1701), *Tables of the Grecian, Roman and Jewish Measures, Weights and Coins* (1705), together with its 1727 revision, *An Argument for Divine Providence* (1710), the *Harvaean Oration* (1727), *An Essay Concerning the Nature of Aliments* (1731), and *An Essay Concerning the Effects of Air on Human Bodies* (1733). These works, so different in tone and polish from the satires usually associated with the doctor's name, show us an entirely new side of the man.

I Of the Laws of Chance

So far as we know, Arbuthnot's first publication appeared in 1692 as a little book entitled *Of the Laws of Chance*, first attributed to him in 1714.[2] The work, as Arbuthnot readily admits, is for the most part a translation of Christiaan Huygens's treatise *De ratiociniis in ludo Aleae*, and he tells us that his writing of the book was more or less a diversion to pass some idle hours and that its purpose was more practical than scholarly:

> *The whole I undertook for my own Divertisement, next to the Satisfaction of some Friends, who would now and then be wrangling about the Proportions of Hazards in some Cases that are here decided. All it required was a few spare Hours, and but little Work for the Brain; my Design in publishing it, was to make it of more general Use, and perhaps persuade a raw Squire, by it, to keep his Money in his Pocket; and if, upon this Account, I should incur the Clamours of the Sharpers, I do not much regard it, since they are a sort of People the World is not bound to provide for.*[3]

In the light of Arbuthnot's own fondness for card games, the writing of this book could hardly have been an onerous task.

Arbuthnot goes on to suggest that games satisfy the human combative instinct and stimulate the mind, for they

> *may be suppos'd to be a tryal of Wit as well as Fortune, and every Man, when he enters the Lists with another, unless out of Complaisance, takes it for granted, his Fortune and Judgment are, at least, equal to those of his Play-Fellows; but this I am sure of, that false Dice, Tricks of Leger-de-main, &c. are inexcusable, for the question in Gaming is not, Who is the best Jugler?* (p. 31)

He insists upon honesty in gaming; men should not be allowed unfair advantages, but they should know how to use probability and mathematics to improve their chances:

> *And it were easy in most Games to make Tables, by Inspection of which, a Man might know what he was either to pay or receive, in any Circumstances you can imagine, it being convenient to save a part of one's Money, rather than venture the loss of it all.* (p. 33)

Such a sensible application of probability, based upon arithmetic and "a few Touches of Algebra," has important implications beyond the card table or the gaming room.

Anticipating the burden of his *Essay on the Usefulness of Mathematical Learning* less than a decade later, Arbuthnot argues that the science of probability can be applied to many more important human concerns:

> *The Reader may here observe the Force of Numbers, which can be successfully applied, even in those things, which one would imagine are subject to no Rules. There are very few things which we know, which are not capable of being reduc'd to a Mathematical Reasoning; and when they cannot, it's a Sign the Knowledge of them is very small and confus'd; and where a Mathematical reasoning can be had, it's as great folly to make use of any other, as to grope for a thing in the Dark, when you have a Candle standing by you.* (p. 31)

The computation of probability might be employed, for example, in politics, though the politician must learn the method through the observation of men and manners and not in the isolation of the study. Arbuthnot's whimsy, however, breaks in for a moment, and he suggests that probability can also be used for making wagers as to the odds on whether a woman will give birth to a son, whether a clergyman in the street is a Nonjuror (one who refused to swear allegiance to William and Mary), whether a woman of age twenty is a virgin (one in ten, says Arbuthnot), or whether a "Town-Spark" of the same age has venereal disease (almost the same odds, he believes) (p. 32).

Arbuthnot then proceeds to set up a series of fourteen propositions to demonstrate the application of his ideas to dice, lotteries, raffles, and whist (pp. 34 - 49). His computations, he says, are not addressed to the mathematician, but to the more general reader (p. 33), though an examination of the propositions and examples suggests that Arbuthnot is a trifle naive in his estimate of his reader's mathematical ability.

The little book on probability is probably of less import than two other books on mathematics that Arbuthnot was to write and publish in the next two decades.

II   An Essay on the Usefulness of Mathematical Learning

His next work, *An Essay on the Usefulness of Mathematical Learning,* was published anonymously in early 1701 with the subtitle "In a Letter from a Gentleman in the City to His Friend at Oxford." In this essay he sets out to show why mathematics has not been a popular intellectual discipline, how a study of mathematics can yield great rewards, and how mathematics is important to many other sciences and even to the arts.

Arbuthnot begins by stating his pleasure at hearing that the "study of the mathematics is promoted and encouraged among the youth of your University" and says, "I have here sent you some short reflections upon the usefulness of mathematical learning, which may serve as an argument to incite you to a closer and more vigorous pursuit of it."[4]

Although mathematics has traditionally been honored with a place among the seven liberal arts, Arbuthnot believes that, for several reasons, this discipline has not been so widely taught or studied as some of the others. First, men are often disinclined to the "serious attention and close arguing" demanded by mathematics. Secondly, they frequently fail to see the relationship of mathematics to other areas of learning. Furthermore, they often surrender to the mistaken belief that the study of this discipline requires a special genius. Finally, there is little public encouragement for such effort, and there are few capable teachers (pp. 409 - 10). And so, Arbuthnot says,

I think I cannot do a better service to learning, youth, and the nation in general, than by shewing that the mathematics of all parts of human knowledge, for the improvement of the mind, for their subserviency to other arts, and their usefulness to the commonwealth, deserve most to be encouraged. (p. 410)

In the remainder of the first half of the essay he proceeds to show the intellectual fruits of mathematical study. Mathematics, he says, makes "the mind attentive to the subjects which it considers"; it also develops a "habit of clear, demonstrative, and methodical reasoning" which "adds a manly vigor to the mind, frees it from prejudice, credulity, and superstition" (pp. 410 - 12). This latter power of mathematics in no way works against religion, though Arbuthnot uncharacteristically digresses to imply that Catholic priests, as in the forced recantation of Galileo, may "exercise their barbarous tyranny over the minds of men." Even so, "truth can never be an enemy to true religion, which appears always to the best advantage when it is most examined" (p. 411).

Arbuthnot sees mathematics as the focus of knowledge, for all of "visible works of God Almighty are made in number, weight, and measure; therefore to consider them we ought to understand arithmetic, geometry, and statics; and the greater advances we make in those arts, the more capable we are of considering such things as are the ordinary objects of our conceptions" (p. 413). Among the scientific disciplines he discusses are astronomy, optics, hydrostatics, paleontology, botany, geography, and chronometry (the latter two being, he says, of great value to the theologian). He shows that mathematics is also important to painting, music, and architecture as well as civil affairs, where mathematical skill is required for finance, planning, coinage and military matters (pp. 413 - 28 *passim*).

To counter the argument that mathematics is too difficult for most students, Arbuthnot says that "the mathematicians have not only invented and ordered all the arts above-mentioned, by which those grand affairs are managed; but have laid down precepts, contrived instruments and abridgments so plainly, that common artificers are capable of practising by them, though they understand not a tittle of the grounds on which the precepts are built" (p. 428).

Therefore, in order to promote the common weal, government must encourage mathematical study and universities must assist in the propagation of this knowledge (pp. 429 - 33). The essay ends with Arbuthnot's suggestions about the pedagogy of mathematics; the study of the subject should involve a large amount of practical demonstration, and a steady and sensible progression from the simple to the complex—from arithmetic to geometry to trigonometry to the more difficult applications in optics, catoptrics, and dioptrics (pp. 433 - 34).

The thrust of the essay, then, is an insistence upon the value of mathematics to the advancement of learning and the relief of human problems. Mathematics, according to Arbuthnot, is an eminently practical study in which the mastery of basic principles supplies a groundwork for so much of intellectual activity. The essay stands in rather bold relief to the satire of corrupt learning in *The Memoirs of Martinus Scriblerus* and *An Essay Concerning the Origin of the Sciences,* where Martin and the other virtuosi run mad in their pride, arrogance, ignorance, and perverted logic. Arbuthnot, as the medical man and mathematician, could see that science might well offer mankind immense benefits. His friends Pope and Swift never seemed to appreciate this fact; the Laputans in Book III of *Gulliver's Travels* represent Swift's view—the ill-fitting clothing and the eccentric houses on the Flying Island are the consequences of an unthinking dependence upon mathematics.

III   An Argument for Divine Providence

A practical application of mathematics is advanced by Arbuthnot in another learned work, *An Argument for Divine Providence, taken from the Constant Regularity observed in the Births of both Sexes* (1710), in which he employs statistics in a kind of argument-by-design to prove the existence and providence of God. The theme of his work is stated in the first paragraph:

Among innumerable Footsteps of Divine Providence to be found in the Works of Nature, there is a very remarkable one to be observed in the exact Ballance that is maintained, between the Numbers of Men and Women; for by this means it is provided, that the Species may never fail, nor perish, since every Male may have its Female, and of a proportionable Age. This Equality of Males and Females is not the Effect of Chance but Divine Providence, working for a good End.[5]

Arbuthnot draws his proof from the so-called "bills," the official statistical summaries of births and deaths, for the years 1629 through 1710, a period of eighty-two years. In each of these years the number of males born exceeds that of females. By employing probability formulas, Arbuthnot shows that such an occurrence (the continued predominance of males in the birth rates) is not the result of chance, but a heavenly providence which works against the accidents to which men are more subject, accidents which

do make a great havock of them, and . . . this loss exceeds far that of the other Sex, occasioned by Diseases incident to it, as Experience convinces us. To repair that Loss, provident Nature, by the disposal of its wise Creator, brings forth more Males than Females; and that in almost constant proportion.[6]

At the end of his essay he attacks polygamy as contrary to the design of nature.

The essay, as Beattie has shown, is not strikingly original in either its methods or its conclusions, for it seems likely that Arbuthnot was heavily indebted to John Graunt's *Natural and Political Observations, Mentioned in a following Index and made upon the Bills of Mortality* (1662).[7] The work by Arbuthnot is not important to the development of either statistical analysis or modern demography, but it does show his continuing fascination with mathematics and its possible applications in the early eighteenth century.

IV   An Examination of Dr. Woodward's Account

Arbuthnot's second published work was *An Examination of Dr. Woodward's Account of the Deluge* (1697). Woodward was a fellow of Gresham College, a layman, and an antiquary who for over a quarter of a century was involved in rancorous controversies with a wide spectrum of intellectuals who often replied to him in the same irascible tone that he employed in his own works. Beattie best summarizes his character:

Woodward was vain, lacked a sense of humor, and had a supreme talent for suspicion. The oil portrait hanging in the Woodwardian Museum at Cambridge reveals a disdainful face; he was imperious, and obviously, like one of Trollope's heroes, had learned to carry his empire in his eye. His quarrels with fellow antiquaries, in and out of the Royal Society, colored the first decade of the new century as he jealously built up his collection and looked with distrust upon anyone who was friendly with Hans Sloane.[8]

During the course of his career he was involved in battles with Sloane (who was a secretary of the Royal Society and a close friend of Arbuthnot), the botanist Dr. Richard Richardson, and many others. Contemporary accounts show his cantankerous nature; C. H. Erndl, a German doctor, said of him, "It is wonderful how chary and churlish he is in showing his cabinet of curiosities. If you do get a peep at it, mind you do not touch the smallest object with so much as the tip of your finger. Nor may you look into a single volume unless he holds it in his own hands."[9] And Zacharias Conrad von Uffenbach, who well knew Woodward's temper, tells of an encounter with the pedant:

Dr. Woodward shewed us all his things with such an affected air and such screwing up of the eyes, that one cannot help laughing; though he suffers you to laugh as little as to speak, requiring every one to listen to him as an oracle, approve and extol all. . . . He repeats whole pages of his works, accompanying them with running panegyrics.[10]

Occasionally Woodward could evoke even stronger reactions, as when, in June 1719, he was attacked with a sword by Dr. Richard Mead (another of Arbuthnot's friends), though the fracas was stopped before Woodward could be injured. At his death Woodward left his collection of fossils to Cambridge University.

Arbuthnot's major confrontation with Woodward occurred after the publication in 1695 of Woodward's *An Essay towards a Natural History of the Earth and Terrestrial Bodies, especially Minerals, as also of the Sea, Rivers, and Springs, with an Account of the Universal Deluge, and of the Effects that it had upon the Earth*. Briefly stated, Woodward's theory was that the earth was originally possessed of a cavity at its center, a void filled with water which erupted at the time of the biblical flood. This deluge dissolved the earth, which was reformed by the settling of soil and shells and other materials; this action would explain, according to Woodward, the existence of fossils with the heaviest at the bottom of the new land-mass.

Arbuthnot's was by no means the first reply to Woodward; in the same year there appeared *Two Essays* by an unidentified "L. P. Master of Arts" and in 1696 Thomas Robinson's *New Observations on the Natural History of this World of Matter, and this World of Life*.

In his *Examination* Arbuthnot seeks to reveal those areas in which Woodward's hypothesis is faulty, but he is also willing to admit that Woodward has made some contributions to scientific knowledge.

He begins by summarizing the argument and details of Woodward's theory and then proceeds to show their inherent fallacies in which the "Alterations of the Earth, here described, appear to be all of them above the Power, and contrary to the Laws of Nature, and consequently exclude the Philosophy of second Causes."[11] The moving of the internal waters to the surface of the earth contradicts the laws of gravity, as do the sinking of objects lighter than water, the dissolution of solids into their constituent parts, and the arrangement of the strata in the manner indicated by Woodward (pp. 201 - 15). Arbuthnot argues not only from contemporary scientific knowledge but also from the natural history found in the Old Testament books of Moses (pp. 216 - 18). Most of the remainder of the *Examination* is devoted to an analysis of suspiciously parallel passages in Woodward's account and Nicolaus Steno's *De Solido Intra Solidum Naturaliter Contento Dissertationis Prodomus* (1699), whose work, according to Woodward's critics, he had misrepresented. Arbuthnot demonstrates the differences in the theories of the two men (pp. 218 - 34).

At the end of his essay Arbuthnot admits that there are some potentially good ideas in Woodward's theory, but suggests that further proof is needed and that Woodward, like others, should be "more diligent in observing, and more cautious in System-making" (p. 234). Those who share Woodward's weaknesses, he says, endanger the credibility of their work, for

First, the World is malicious, and when they write for an Opinion it spoils the Credit of their Observations. They have then taken their Party, and may be suspected for partial Witnesses. In the next Place, Mankind, in these Matters, is naturally too rash, and apt to put more in the Conclusion than there is in the Premises. Yes, some there are so fond of an Opinion, that they will take Pleasure to cheat themselves, and would bring every Thing to fit their Hypothesis. Then only may we expect to succeed in compiling of Theories, when we build upon true and decisive Observations; and survey the Works of Nature with the same Geometry (tho' in a more imperfect Degree) by which the divine Architect put them together. (pp. 234 - 35)

This statement reflects Arbuthnot's rationality and his belief that in scientific investigation theory must follow from reliable and well-tested evidence, a belief that places him squarely in the tradition and the spirit of the great scientists of the age. Like Swift in the digression on madness (Section IX) in *A Tale of a Tub* and Pope in

An Essay on Man, Arbuthnot is deeply distrustful of systems-makers; for all three writers such men violate common sense and the true spirit of learning.

Arbuthnot's *Examination of Dr. Woodward's Account of the Deluge* shows him at his best in his scientific writing, for the argument is careful and well ordered, the style fluent and graceful, and the spirit relatively non-partisan. But by the time of the gathering of the wits in the Scriblerus circle of 1713 - 1714, Arbuthnot's attitude toward Woodward would be hardened and thus take its expression in satire.

V Tables of . . . Measures, Weights and Coins

Arbuthnot's far-ranging intellectual interests are further demonstrated in his *Tables of the Grecian, Roman and Jewish Measures, Weights and Coins* (1705), which was later expanded into *Tables of Ancient Coins, Weights and Measures, Explained and Exemplified in Several Dissertations,* published in 1727. Neither work is distinguished by originality or style, and Arbuthnot obviously drew a good share of his material for the revision from Bishop George Hooper's book of 1721, *An Inquiry into the State of the Ancient Measures, the Attick, the Roman, and especially the Jewish.*[12]

Today Arbuthnot's work on coins and measures seems to be of little value, as Beattie has shown in his discussion of the book's reputation, which has had a mixed history.[13] Indeed, Arbuthnot himself did not think very highly of it, as he tells us in his preface:

The Faults (of which I am sensible there are a great many) are in some measure owing to my want of Leisure. . . . The Mistakes are easily corrected from the Principles and Materials contain'd in the Book it self. . . . It is the Product of Labour more than Judgment, consisting chiefly of Collections from several Authors, and for which I am obliged to Hostus's Historia Rei Nummariae. I propose no Reputation by it, and I hope I shall lose none.[14]

He goes on to forestall the expected criticism by professional scholars:

With great Submission I deprecate the Wrath of all Criticks and Antiquaries, which is wont to be very flagrant on such Occasions. I do not value my self on my Skill either in Languages, History or Antiquity; far less on the little Skill in Numbers which is demanded for the whole Performance, which bating one Problem about Interest, requires no depth of Calculation. I question not but any of them would have executed this Work better than my self. Besides, I have hardly Courage, I am sure not Leisure, to defend my self. [15]

For the most part the book is a loose and disjointed compendium of facts and generalizations by which he moves from one topic to another, often without much attention to either progression or transition, from coinage through medicine, climate, and navigation. As such the book has little value to the general reader. Arbuthnot was not a professional in any of these areas except medicine, and being about sixty when the amplified edition appeared in 1727, at a time when he was suffering ailments incident to age, he possessed neither the vitality, the interest, the leisure, nor the expertise to produce a better book. Both books smack too much of the study, where Arbuthnot seems never to have been comfortable, preferring the company of his family and friends and finding his talents best fulfilled in satire and conversation.

VI   *Three Medical Works*

The remaining books produced by Arbuthnot during the last decade of his life have to do with his own professional interests. In 1727 he delivered the *Oratio Anniversaria Harvaeana* at the College of Physicians in London, and in 1731 there appeared *An Essay Concerning the Nature of Aliments,* followed by *An Essay Concerning the Effects of Air on Human Bodies.*

The Harvaean lecture, delivered in Latin, was one of the highest honors that could be given to an English physician. Intended to commemorate William Harvey, who had published his theory of the circulation of the blood in 1628, had been elected president of the College of Physicians (though he declined to serve), and had given the College various gifts, the oration was an acknowledgment of the lecturer's achievements. Arbuthnot had been chosen an Elect of the College on October 5, and he read his oration on October 18.

In his lecture Arbuthnot discusses the evolution and history of medical science from its early connections with superstition through the emergence of modern medicine in the seventeenth century. He praises the work of Hippocrates for his classification of diseases, symptoms, and cures. He goes on to show that in succeeding ages medicine made slow progress until the Renaissance, when Henry

VIII chartered the Royal College of Physicians at the suggestion of Thomas Linacre, and when Englishmen such as John Caius (founder of Caius College, Cambridge), Richard Caldwall, Theodore Gulston, Thomas Sydenham, and Baldwin Hamey did much to advance English medicine. After glorifying Harvey, whose theory had been the most important medical discovery of the seventeenth century, Arbuthnot examines various aspects of the contemporary medical scene and points out the need to employ such new discoveries as the microscope in research, to collect climatological data for the study of disease, and to use autopsies to extend the boundaries of medical science.

Serious in tone, as appropriate for the occasion, the oration has occasional touches of lightness, and it is graceful and learned. Given his conviviality and his sense of humor, Arbuthnot might well have been one of the great teachers at either of the two universities.

Arbuthnot's next medical work, *An Essay Concerning the Nature of Aliments, and the Choice of Them, According to the Different Constitutions of Human Bodies,* was also written during the years when his health was failing and was published at the suggestion of some friends, as he tells us in the preface:

The Circumstances of ill Health, and Absence from my Books in which I compos'd it, and the Want of Leisure since to correct it sufficiently, may be some Excuse for the Want of that Accuracy which the Subject deserves. . . . I am likewise obliged to make use of a very common and trivial Reason for publishing it at this Time, viz. The Approbation of some Friends who perus'd it, and persuaded me that it might be of some Use to the Publick.[16]

In 1732 Arbuthnot published a second and expanded edition to which was appended a set of dietary rules. The whole work, as is typical of most of Arbuthnot's writing, is orderly, clear, and informative. It is aimed at the common reader, not the medical specialist, for anyone "with as much Anatomy as a Butcher knows, and moderate Skill in Mechanicks, may understand the whole Essay, provided he goes through it at Leisure, and with Attention."[17]

The thrust of the book is to discuss the influence of various types of food on human health, as well as the relationship of climate and the seasons to the body. At times it is technical and prolix, and it did not contribute much to the advancement of medical knowledge, but its numerous editions in Great Britain, France, and Germany indicate that it enjoyed something of a minor reputation.

His final book on medicine, *An Essay Concerning the Effects of Air on Human Bodies*, seems to have suffered from the same fatigue, illness, and lack of attention which attended the essay on aliments. Writing at a time when the effects of air and the processes of respiration and osmosis were not fully understood, Arbuthnot based much of this treatise on the experiments of Hermann Boerhaave, Robert Boyle, Stephen Hales, James Keill, and Thomas Sydenham as reported in the *Philosophical Transactions* of the Royal Society. As Beattie has observed, "Arbuthnot was alive to what had been discovered; but the reasoning is always his own, and he frequently reverts to the need of better observation before conclusions can be drawn."[18] But the book is flawed by his assumption of some of the popular medical ideas of the day—that air can be polluted by exhalations of the lungs and that air is the cause of refrigeration. He did, however, contribute one interesting speculation in his chapter on pestilential fevers, where he describes the "cattarhous fever," its spread within several countries, its symptoms and remedies, and its causes, a discussion which, as Charles Creighton believes, was significant:

Although Arbuthnot was hardly a serious epidemiologist, any more than Boyle, yet in the growth of opinion on the subject of morbific matters in the air, he may be said to have shifted the interest from inorganic or mineral substances and gases, to organic matters chiefly of human or animal origin, and from the deeper regions of the globe, such as only earthquakes reach, to the surface stratum of soil and subsoil which is affected by every rise and fall of the ground-water.[19]

One of the more interesting speculations in the book is Arbuthnot's suggestion that climate operates upon the minds, emotions, and language of human beings, a theory which he had previously used for satiric effect in *The History of John Bull:*

It seems agreeable to Reason and Experience, that the Air operates sensibly in forming the Constitutions of Mankind, the Specialties of Features, Complexion, Temper, and consequently the Manners of Mankind, which are found to vary much in different Countries and Climates. . . . People of delicate Nerves and moveable Spirits are often joyful, sullen, sprightly, dejected, hopeful, despairing, according to the Weather; and these Changes happen, but pass unobserv'd in stronger Constitutions. . . . The

serrated close way of Speaking of Northern Nations, may be owing to their
Reluctance to open their Mouth wide in cold Air, which must make their
Language abound in Consonants, whereas from a contrary Cause, the
Inhabitants of warmer Climates opening their Mouths, must form a softer
Language, abounding in Vowels.[20]

Arbuthnot also attributes the technological and speculative
superiority of the northern nations and the aesthetic dominance of
the southern to the influence of climate, the former being
stimulated by the cold, the latter by the warm. He extends the influence of climate to government, suggesting that cold weather,
requiring greater labor for the acquisition of property, causes people
to be less tolerant of tyranny, though he admits that social pressures
and ideas may also exert strong pressures on the evolution of
government.[21]

VII   *"Great and Various Erudition"*

When Lord Chesterfield spoke of Arbuthnot as a man of "great
and various erudition," he may in part have been alluding to the
scientific works discussed in this chapter, though he was also undoubtedly thinking of the satires. As we examine Arbuthnot's
writing on learned subjects, we find him to be something of a dilettante, a man trained in medicine and mathematics whose mind
ranged widely over other areas—geology, diet, coinage, climate—which were somewhat tangential to his own specialty. So far
as we know, Arbuthnot did little or no research on his own, being
content to assimilate the theories and experiments of earlier scientists and those of his contemporaries and to subject these findings to
his own experience and common sense. Thus he embodied much of
the best in the intellectual tradition of his time.

As we have seen in the chapters on his satires, Arbuthnot could
look at his own profession and the scientific world in general with
ironic detachment. The scientific satire in *The Memoirs of Martinus
Scriblerus* is undoubtedly his, and he must have enjoyed Swift's jabs
at the virtuosi in Book III of *Gulliver's Travels* (and perhaps even
the satire on physicians in Book IV). Though much more sympathetic to experiment and theory than was Swift, he could both see
the failings of many of his contemporaries and yet appreciate the
purpose and potential of the science of his time.

CHAPTER 7

Epilogue: "The Excellence of His Heart"

THE preceding chapters of this study have traced the course of Arbuthnot's career and his literary friendships, and examined the works ascribed to him by scholarly consensus. The life and writings of the doctor reveal a man who moved with ease among the greatest figures—literary, political, and scientific—of his age and made valuable contributions to the literature of the first third of the eighteenth century and to what many regard as the golden age of English satire.

We know a great deal about Arbuthnot: his relationships with Pope, Swift, and Gay; his writing of various literary and scientific works; his participation in the intellectual and personal controversies of his time. Nevertheless we do not possess the abundance of information that we have for his more famous colleagues. Very little, as we have seen, is known about the first three decades of his career, and little more is likely to come to light to supplement the relatively few facts that we already have. Even in the later stages of his work, when he spent some time at court and in the company of the great Augustan writers, we have only sizable fragments, the most significant of which are contained in Angus Ross's fine unpublished edition of the letters.

Furthermore, there is a singular lack of extensive scholarly work on Arbuthnot. There is no modern and reliable collection of his works; indeed none of his individual works is available in twentieth-century editions except *The Memoirs of Martinus Scriblerus* and *The History of John Bull* (and these only in expensive volumes). And except for Lester Beattie's excellent book (to which all students of Arbuthnot will remain indebted for a long time to come) there are in print no extensive studies of the man, his work, and his in-

120

tellectual and literary relationships. As for articles in professional journals, the field is similarly sparse.

Badly needed are a scholarly edition of Arbuthnot's works and studies of his relationships with the major Augustans—particularly Swift, Gay, and Pope— and with the important figures in the courts of Queen Anne and King George I. Nor has his career as a physician been adequately examined in the light of eighteenth-century medical theory and practice. And, finally, we need an analysis of the twenty or so pieces assigned to Arbuthnot by various eighteenth-century editors and publishers, works which modern scholars have generally doubted as being his.[1] A closer study of these works, which appeared as early as 1714 and as late as a few days before his death in 1735, might not provide any more definitive answers to the question of Arbuthnot's possible authorship, but it might well broaden our understanding of the period in which he wrote.

The fact that these probably spurious pieces could be passed off as his in the several decades following his death further testifies to Arbuthnot's literary reputation in the eighteenth century. As we have seen in Chapter 1, he was highly thought of by his contemporaries. Gay, for example, in his "Prologue" to *The Shepherd's Week* (1714), could celebrate his friend's expert medical service to the ailing queen:

> A skilful Leach, (so God him speed)
> They said has wrought this blessed Deed,
> This Leach *Arbuthnot* was yclept
> Who many a Night not once had slept;
> But watch'd our gracious Sov'raign still,
> For who cou'd rest when she was ill?
> Oh, may'st thou henceforth sweetly sleep.
> Sheer, Swains, oh sheer your softest Sheep
> To swell his Couch; for well I wean,
> He sav'd the Realm who sav'd the Queen.[2]

And Arbuthnot's reputation remained equally high during the remainder of the eighteenth century. John Boyle, fifth earl of Orrery, writing in his *Remarks on the Life and Writings of Jonathan Swift* (1752), gives strong praise to both the man and the writer:

Although he was justly celebrated for wit and learning, there was an excellence in his character more amiable than all his other qualifications: I mean the excellence of his heart. He has shewed himself equal to any of his contemporaries in humour and vivacity: and he was superior to most men in acts of humanity and benevolence: his very sarcasms are the satirical strokes of good-nature; they are like flaps of the face given in jest, tthe effects of which may raise blushes, but no blackness will appear after the blows. . . . He is seldom serious, except in his attacks upon vice, and then his spirit rises with a manly strength, and a noble indignation. . . . No man exceeded him in the moral duties of life: a merit still more to his honour, as the ambitious powers of wit and genius are seldom submissive enough to confine themselves within the limitations of morality.[3]

Even later in the century, the poet William Cowper, writing to the Reverend William Unwin on March 21, 1784, and speaking of Johnson's *Lives of the Poets*, says that "one might search these eight volumes with a candle, as the prophet says, to find a man, and not find one, unless, perhaps, Arbuthnot were he."[4] And in his *Table Talk* (1782), when speaking of the "constellation" of Augustan wits (including Addison and Pope), he links Arbuthnot with Swift:

> Nature imparting her satiric gift,
> Her serious mirth, to Arbuthnot and Swift,
> With droll sobriety they rais'd a smile
> At Folly's cost, themselves unmov'd the while.
> That constellation set, the world in vain
> Must hope to look upon their like again.[5]

In the nineteenth century, however, his reputation quickly declined, and except for several comments by William Makepeace Thackeray (to be quoted later) he appears in literary discussions only as the satellite of Swift, Gay, and Pope.

The twentieth-century critics and historians have almost totally ignored him. George Sherburn's brief comments in Albert C. Baugh's *A Literary History of England* are typical of the very generalized attention given Arbuthnot in our own time:

It [the early eighteenth-century pamphlet] loved ingenuity, and rose to allegorical excellence in the masterpiece of Dr. John Arbuthnot (1667 - 1735), now known as *The History of John Bull.* . . . "John Bull" as symbolizing England is Arbuthnot's invention.[6]

One would prefer to see a more sympathetic treatment, more extended, more filled with insight, as in Hugh Walker's discussion in *English Satire and Satirists:*

There is "no brother near the throne" of Jonathan Swift: he is unrivalled among English prose satirists. Yet there is one, a contemporary and friend, perhaps nearly equal to him in native gifts, and incomparably more amiable and attractive. This was John Arbuthnot (1667 - 1735), the foremost physician of his time, immortalised by Pope's famous epistle, a piece honourable alike to him who sent and to him who received. If Swift was in some aspects almost inhuman, Arbuthnot was both eminently human and humane. No one was ever less troubled than he with the *cacoethes scribendi*, no one ever showed less of literary jealousy. His writings are of considerable volume, but they were penned because he had knowledge to convey or thoughts to express, not because he desired fame as an author. To that he was so indifferent as to leave his works for which he is now best remembered mixed up with those of Swift and Pope. . . .[7]

Unfortunately, except for a handful of doctoral dissertations, there seems to be little interest in Arbuthnot at the present. He has become, like Sir William Temple, one of those interesting background figures who stand at the edges of the portraits of the major writers in the eighteenth century, a man to be deferred to with a passing and ingratiating remark—and then ignored.

A more reasonable view is that Arbuthnot is a man well worth reading in his own right—not as a possible source for *Gulliver's Travels*, not as a friend and confidant of Swift and Pope, and not just as the writer of *The History of John Bull*, fruitful as these ventures may be—but as a writer, thinker, and professional man who lived in times that were intellectually, socially, and politically exciting. Certainly there are few ambiguities or rhetorical complexities that commend some authors to modern critics, but there is an abundance of challenging and enlightening material for the more catholic reader as well as a great deal that offers an insight into the early eighteenth century. Although primarily a physician, Arbuthnot, as we have seen, had a lively concern with literature, politics, and science, a concern reflected in both his major and minor works, several of which ought to be included in eighteenth-century anthologies, but are not.

As a summary of Arbuthnot's career, we should look at what was his last work, a poem written and published a short time before his death, a poem, which though echoing certain parts of Pope's *Essay on Man*, expresses his view of mankind and the world. "ΓΝΑΘΙ ΣΕΑΥΤΟΝKnow Thyself" was published at London in 1734 with an advertisement by Arbuthnot: "The following poem was wrote several years ago; as it may do good to some, and cannot hurt the reputation of the author, though he should be known, I have given it to my bookseller to publish. It contains some thoughts of Monsieur Pascal, which cannot make it less acceptable to the public."[8] This poem, oddly enough, is the only work of Arbuthnot's which we have in manuscript.[9] The printed version runs to 137 lines, while the manuscript has only 128, and Beattie suggests that the changes and additions "probably represent revision by a skilled hand, perhaps that of Pope."[10] The published text, since it probably represents Arbuthnot's final statement, will be used in the following discussion.

Arbuthnot opens his poem with a long series of questions regarding the place of man in the universe:

> What am I? how produced? and for what end?
> Whence drew I being? to what period tend?
> Am I the abandoned orphan of blind chance?
> Dropt by wild atoms in disordered dance?
> Or from an endless chain of causes wrought?
> And of unthinking substance, born with thought?
> By motion which began without a cause,
> Supremely wise, without design or laws.
> Am I but what I seem, mere flesh and blood;
> A branching channel, with a mazy flood? (p. 436)

Thus begins his analysis of the human condition, an examination which denies chance or purely natural processes as the origin of man.

Arbuthnot admits that man is the product of earthly elements but claims that he also partakes of the divine, a duality which frustrates his extreme ambitions and causes him no end of intellectual restlessness:

> . . . I own a mother, earth,
> But claim superior lineage by my Sire,
> Who warmed the unthinking clod with heavenly fire:
> Essence divine, with lifeless clay allayed,
> By double nature, double instinct swayed. (pp. 436 - 37)

Man is unable to rise above his human condition, finding himself "Tied to this massy globe with magic chain." He looks about him for solutions to the riddle of his nature, seeking answers in the movements of the heavenly bodies and the insects:

> Some beastly want, craving, importunate,
> Vile as the grinning mastiffs at my gate,
> Calls off from heavenly truth this reasoning me,
> And tells me I'm a brute as much as he. (p.437)

Wherever he looks, man "Sees he's a king, but 'tis a king desposed." And when he turns to other men for answers, he is told by one, "Thou art a god," and by another called "thou two-legged beast" (pp. 437, 438).

The answer, Arbuthnot believes, is not in man's own power but in Scripture, "The balm, the light, the guide of souls perplexed." In imagery reminiscent of Dryden's *Religio Laici*, he says that through scriptural revelation,

> . . . the benighted traveller that strays
> Through doubtful paths, enjoys the morning rays;
> The nightly mist, and thick descending dew,
> Parting, unfold the fields and vaulted blue. (p. 438)

The systems of the philosophers offer little in the way of either enlightenment or consolation, especially those of the Stoics and the Epicureans:

> Zeno's were vain, vain Epicurus' schemes,
> Their systems false, delusive were their dreams;
> Unskilled my twofold nature to divide,
> One nursed by pleasure, and one nursed by pride. (p. 438)

God cannot be blamed for man's estate, since He created him faultless and with free will; thus man alone is responsible for his own condition:

> Born on thy new-imped wings, thou took'st thy flight,
> Left thy Creator, and the realms of light;
> Disdained this gentle precept to fulfil;
> And though to grow a god by doing ill. (p. 439)

Thus man remains mixed in his nature—"Angel enough to seek thy bliss again,/ And brute enough to make thy search in vain." In his rejection of the traditional philosophies, as Beattie has shown, Arbuthnot follows Pascal's *Entretien de Pascal avec Saci* (1728),[11] but this distrust of the philosophers is also to be found in the major figures of the Restoration and eighteenth century—Dryden (*Religio Laici*), Pope (*An Essay on Man*), and Swift (*A Tale of a Tub* and *Gulliver's Travels*), to name only the more obvious.

At the end of the poem Arbuthnot finds hope and meaning in a traditional Christian resignation and faith:

> Return, and seek thy father, and thy God:
> Yet think not to regain thy native sky,
> Born on the wings of vain philosophy;
> Mysterious passage! hid from human eyes;
> Soaring you'll sink, and sinking you will rise:
> Let humble thoughts thy wary footsteps guide,
> Regain by meekness what you lost by pride. (p. 439)

Thus man is incapable of achieving perfect happiness through the operation of his reason and his earthly nature; only through humility and divine grace can he achieve that state.

The ideas of the poem are not original, and the often cramped and sluggish couplets make it clear that Arbuthnot had little talent as a poet. The attacks upon the moral philosophers, the skepticism toward reason as a source of happiness, the concept of man as a mixed being aspiring to the heavens but finding his wings overburdened by his worldly nature, the counsel to faith and resignation—these are the commonplaces of the age from Dryden to Samuel Johnson. Arbuthnot shares Pope's view that man is

> Plac'd on this isthmus of a middle state,
> A being darkly wise, and rudely great:
> With too much knowledge for the Sceptic side,
> With too much weakness for the Stoic's pride,
> He hangs between; in doubt to act, or rest,
> In doubt to deem himself a God, or Beast;
> In doubt his Mind or Body to prefer,
> Born but to die, and reas'ning but to err;
> Alike in ignorance, his reason such,
> Whether he thinks too little, or too much:
> Chaos of Thought and Passion, all confus'd;
> Still by himself abus'd, or disabus'd.[12]

In the end, for Pope, "VIRTUE only makes our Bliss below; / And all our Knowledge is, OURSELVES TO KNOW."[13] The fact that

An Essay on Man was published in 1733 - 1734 strongly suggests the influence of Pope.

As imitative as Arbuthnot's poem is, it nevertheless is of a piece with the rest of his work, reflecting his distrust of the intellectuals as found in *The Memoirs of Martinus Scriblerus* and the other satires on corrupt learning, his belief in the efficacy of the active life which permeated his relationships with friends and colleagues, and his implicit confidence (as seen in his scientific works) that there is much man can do, within the limitations of his own God-given abilities, to relieve his estate in this world. The poem, then, is Arbuthnot's final statement on mankind and the world.

Viewed from the distance of almost three centuries, the life and work of Dr. Arbuthnot at first glance seem to be those of a man on the periphery of the great, one who is better known for his relationships to the famous than for his own work. Something there was about Arbuthnot which made him careless about his own fame ("I propose no reputation"), a cast of mind which caused him to write his works and then often leave them both unrevised and anonymous. When we think of Arbuthnot, we do not find ourselves fascinated by stories of intense personal antagonisms (as in the case of Swift and Pope), by deep involvement in politics (as with Steele, Swift, or Defoe), by the brilliant and witty world of Chesterfield, or by the tremendous literary achievements of his more famous contemporaries. Instead we think of the capable and humane physician, the writer of learned books on various subjects, and the gentle satirist. If there is another Augustan who reminds us of Arbuthnot, it is Gay. Both were intimates of Swift and Pope; both failed to win the literary prominence of their two friends; and both owe their modern reputations largely to one work, *The History of John Bull* in the case of Arbuthnot, and *The Beggar's Opera* in that of Gay.

But Arbuthnot is still worthy of study. A reading of his letters tells us a good deal about his friendships with the great and near-great of the early eighteenth century and the day-to-day affairs of a man of letters and medicine. His *History of John Bull* is an amusing satire on the particulars of Augustan politics and the universal tragicomedy of war, peace, and religion. Whatever parts of *The Memoirs of Martinus Scriblerus* are his (and many seem to be) reflect the timeless frailties of the scholar and intellectual. And to a great degree his works prove the sometimes-forgotten truism that the minor works of a culture may tell us as much, if not more, about that time and place than do the writings of the better known.

Physician, mathematician, satirist, and trusted friend, Dr. John Arbuthnot was precisely what the Victorian novelist Thackeray called him: "a man remarkable for his benevolence as well as his wit," and "one of the wisest, wittiest, most accomplished, gentlest of mankind."[14] A decent and reasonable man could ask for no higher praise.

Notes and References

1. G. A. Aitken, *The Life and Works of John Arbuthnot* (Oxford: Clarendon Press, 1892; New York: Russell & Russell, 1968), pp. 1 - 7 *passim*. Aitken also includes a genealogical table and notes, pp. 172 - 75. See also Lester M. Beattie, *John Arbuthnot, Mathematician and Satirist* (Cambridge: Harvard University Press, 1935; New York: Russell & Russell, 1967), pp. 409 - 10, and Angus Ross, ed., *The Correspondence of Dr. John Arbuthnot* (Unpublished Ph. D. dissertation, Cambridge University, 1956), pp. 17 - 21.

2. Aitken, pp. 7, 10, 18; Beattie, pp. 4 - 5; Ross, pp. 21 - 23.

3. Swift, *Journal to Stella.*, ed. Harold Williams (Oxford: Clarendon Press, 1948), I, 219 - 20. Other references to Arbuthnot abound in the two volumes of the *Journal*. The variant spellings and pronunciations of Arbuthnot's name are discussed by Beattie, pp. 410 - 11.

4. *Journal to Stella*, I, 329.

5. Swift, *Correspondence*, ed. Harold Williams (Oxford: Clarendon Press, 1963 - 1965), II, 34 - 37.

6. *Ibid.*, V, 63. Gay died in late 1732.

7. Swift, *Poems*, ed. Harold Williams (Oxford: Clarendon Press, 1958), II, 555.

8. *Journal to Stella*, I, 356.

9. Aitken, pp. 48n., 60n., 75 - 77.

10. Beattie, pp. 20 - 32 *passim*.

11. *Ibid.*, pp. 30 - 31.

12. *Ibid.*, pp. 17 - 20 *passim*.

13. *Ibid.*, pp. 8 - 17 *passim;* Aitken, pp. 36 - 37.

14. For a comprehensive history and discussion of the Scriblerus Club, see Charles Kerby-Miller, ed., *Memoirs of the Extraordinary Life, Works, and Discoveries of Martinus Scriblerus* (New Haven: Yale University Press, 1950; New York: Russell & Russell, 1966), pp. 1 - 84; see also Robert J. Allen, *The Clubs of Augustan London* (Cambridge: Harvard University Press, 1933), pp. 260 - 83, and George Sherburn, *The Early Career of Alexander Pope* (Oxford: Clarendon Press, 1934), pp. 69 - 82.

15. Joseph Spence, *Anecdotes, Observations, and Characters, of Books and Men*, ed. Samuel Weller Singer, 2nd edition (London: John Russell Smith, 1858), p. 8.

16. Swift, *Corespondence*, II, 46.

17. Both Aitken, p. 95, and Beattie, p. 256, are uncertain about ascribing either pamphlet to Arbuthnot.

18. Pope, *Correspondence*, ed. George Sherburn (Oxford: Clarendon Press, 1956), II, 133.

19. *Ibid.*, p. 60.

20. *Ibid.*, p. 322.

21. Gay, *Letters*, ed. C. F. Burgess (Oxford: Clarendon Press, 1966), p. 49.

22. Beattie, pp. 348 - 50, cites contemporary as well as recent discussions of Arbuthnot's shortcomings as an antiquarian.

23. Pope, *Correspondence*, III, 59n., 106n., 114.

24. Quoted in Aitken, p. 146.

25. Pope, *Correspondence*, III, p. 417.

26. Swift, *Correspondence*, IV, pp. 256 - 57.

27. Pope, *Correspondence*, III, p. 417.

28. Swift, *Correspondence*, IV, pp. 300, 334.

29. See Aitken, pp. 12 - 18, 22 - 24. 27, 28, 31 - 33, 50 *passim*, for some of Arbuthnot's correspondence with Charlett. The letters are also contained in Ross's edition.

30. *Ibid.*, p. 24.

31. *Ibid.*, p. 40.

32. Pope, *Correspondence*, II, p. 253.

33. Boswell, *The Life of Samuel Johnson*, ed. George Birbeck Hill, rev. L. F. Powell (Oxford: Clarendon Press, 1934 - 50), II, p. 372.

34. As quoted in Aitken, p. 19.

35. As quoted in Aitken, pp. 31 - 33.

36. Swift, *Correspondence*, II, p. 303.

37. As quoted in Aitken, p. 55.

38. *The Letters of Philip Dormer Stanhope, Earl of Chesterfield*, ed. Lord Mahon (London: Richard Bentley, 1845), II, pp. 446 - 48 *passim*.

39. Pope, *Imitations of Horace and Epistle to Dr Arbuthnot and the Epilogue to the Satires*, ed. John Butt, in *The Twickenham Edition of the Poems of Alexander Pope* (London: Methuen; New Haven:·Yale University Press, 1939), IV, p. 127.

40. Pope, *Correspondence*, II, p. 253.

41. Swift, *Correspondence*, III, p. 104.

42. Pope, *Correspondence*, II, p. 395.

43. As quoted in Aitken, p. 134.

44. As quoted in Beattie, p. 337.

45. As quoted in Aitken, p. 134n.

Chapter Two

1. The history of England's relationships with Scotland from 1660 to about 1714 is discussed by Sir George Clark, *The Later Stuarts, 1660 - 1714*, 2nd edition (Oxford: Clarendon Press 1955), pp. 263 - 93.

2. Aitken, pp. 396 - 97. All references to the *Sermon* and to *The Art of Political Lying*, except where noted, will be to Aitken's edition and will be cited internally.

3. *Journal to Stella*, ed. Williams, II, p. 562.

4. *Ibid.*, p. 579.

5. As quoted in Beattie, p. 293. Aitken uses the reprint of 1727, which eliminates the names of the two political parties and thus dulls the cutting edge of the satire against the Whigs.

6. Beattie, pp. 293 - 94.

7. Aitken, p. 75. All references cited internally are to this edition.

8. *The Prose Works of Jonathan Swift*, ed. Herbert Davis (Oxford: B. H. Blackwell, 1939 - 1968), XI, p. 238.

9. *The Tatler*, ed. G. A. Aitken (London: Duckworth, 1899), I, p. 91; III, pp. 218 - 22; III, pp. 244 - 47; III, pp. 332 - 37; IV, pp. 185 - 89. *The Spectator*, ed. Donald F. Bond (Oxford: Clarendon Press, 1965), V, pp. 136 - 37. Pope, *Poems* (Twickenham edition), V, p. 290.

10. See Lester M. Beattie, "The Authorship of *The Quidnuncki's*," *Modern Philology*, XXX (1933), 317 - 20.

11. Swift, *Poems*, III, pp. 1121 - 22.

12. *Ibid.*, p. 1122.

13. *Ibid.*

14. *The Spectator*, ed. Bond, V, pp. 136 - 37. See also *The Tatler*, Number 10 (ed. Aitken, I, p. 91): "The insignificancy of my manners to the rest of the world makes the laughers call me *quidnunc*, a phrase I shall never enquire what they mean by it."

15. *The Tatler*, ed. Aitken, III p. 335.

16. *Ibid.*, III, pp. 218 - 22, 244 - 47, 332 - 37; IV, pp. 185 - 89. For a brief history of the newsmonger in eighteenth-century satire, see Richmond P. Bond, *The Tatler: The Makings of a Literary Journal* (Cambridge: Harvard University Press, 1971), pp. 147 - 49.

17. Pope, *Poems* (Twickenham edition), III:ii, pp. 83 - 84.

18. Swift, *Poems*, II, pp. 519, 560.

19. Sandra Lee Kerman, ed., "Francis Charteris, Convicted of Using Violence to the Person of Ann Bond," *The Newgate Calendar, or Malefactor's Bloody Register* (New York: Capricorn Books, 1962), pp. 114 - 21. This collection was first published in 1771.

20. Beattie, p. 303n.

21. Aitken, pp. 317 - 18. The epitaph is also reprinted in the Twickenham edition of Pope's *Poems*, III: ii, p. 84.

22. *The Newgate Calendar*, ed. Kerman, p. 121.

23. Pope, *Correspondence*, III, p 417.

Chapter Three

1. Kenneth Hopkins, "John Bull," *Encyclopaedia Britannica*, 1965 ed., XIII, pp. 37 - 38.

2. Herman Teerink, editor of *The History of John Bull* (Amsterdam: H.

J. Paris, 1925), pp. 82 - 131, believes that Swift, not Arbuthnot, was the author. Teerink's conclusion, based on tenuous internal evidence, has been demolished by Beattie, pp. 36 - 58. See also Arthur W. Secord, *American Historical Review*, XXXII (January 1927), 357, and Edith J. Morley, *The Year's Work in English Studies*, VI (1925), 220, both of whom support Teerink; and Émile Pons, *Revue Anglo-Américaine*, IV (April 1927), 354, and Thomas F. Mayo, *PMLA*, XLV (March 1930), 274, who attack Teerink's theory. The definitive discussion of the problem is Alan W. Bower and Robert A. Erickson, eds., *The History of John Bull* (Oxford: Clarendon Press, 1976), pp. xxii - xxxviii.

3. For a discussion of the domestic and foreign implications of the War of the Spanish Succession, see Sir George Clark, *The Later Stuarts, 1660 - 1714*, 2nd edition (Oxford: Clarendon Press, 1955), pp. 200 - 48; and G. M. Trevelyan, *England under Queen Anne* (London: Longmans, Green and Co., 1930 - 34), all three volumes.

4. Ivor F. Burton, *The Captain General: The Career of John Churchill, Duke of Marlborough, 1702 - 1711* (London: Constable and Co., 1968), p. 163.

5. Bower and Erickson, p. 9. All references to *The History of John Bull* in this chapter are to this edition and will be cited internally. Arbuthnot's theory of climatic influence can be traced back through Sir William Temple (*Of Poetry* and *An Essay upon the Original and Nature of Government*) and Milton (*Areopagitica* and *History of Britain*), as well as other Renaissance writers, to Aristotle's *Poetics*. See Z. S. Fink, *Modern Language Quarterly*, II (1941), 67 - 80, and Thomas B. Stroup, *Modern Language Quarterly*, IV (1943), 185 - 89.

6. Teerink, p. 141n.

7. Swift, *Poems*, ed. Williams, I, pp. 296 - 97.

8. Burton (note 4 *supra*); Winston Churchill, *Marlborough, His Life and Times*, 4 vols. (London: G. G. Harrap, 1933 - 1938); David Green, *Sarah Duchess of Marlborough* (New York: Charles Scribner's Sons, 1967).

9. Patricia Köster, "Swift, Arbuthnot, and the Law," *American Notes and Queries*, IV:6 (February 1969), 83 - 84, and Richard H. Passon, "Legal Satire in *Gulliver* from *John Bull*," *American Notes and Queries*, V (1967), 99 - 100, comment upon Arbuthnot's satire on law.

10. See Patricia Köster, "Arbuthnot's Use of Quotation and Parody in His Account of the Sacheverell Affair," *Philological Quarterly*, XLVIII (1969), 201 - 11.

11. Swift, *Prose Works*, ed. Davis, XI, p. 55.

12. See William P. Holden, *Anti-Puritan Satire, 1572 - 1700* (New Haven: Yale University Press, 1954), for a discussion of literary attacks on Puritanism before 1700.

13. A concise and clear account of the controversy over occasional conformity can be found in Henry W. Clark, *History of English Nonconformi-*

ty (London, 1911; reprinted New York: Russell and Russell, 1965), II, pp. 145 - 54.

14. For the continuations and imitations of John Bull, see Beattie, pp. 161 - 89.

Chapter Four

1. As quoted in Charles Kerby-Miller, ed., *The Memoirs of Martinus Scriblerus* (New Haven: Yale University Press, 1950; New York: Russell & Russell, 1966), p. vii.

2. Pope, *Correspondence*, I, p. 195.

3. *Spectator*, No. 457, August 14, 1712.

4. *Memoirs of Martinus Scriblerus*, ed. Kerby-Miller, p. 15. Henceforward cited as *Memoirs*.

5. Swift, *Poems*, I, p. 185.

6. Swift, *Correspondence*, II, p. 46.

7. *Memoirs*, p. 58.

8. *Ibid.*, pp. 59 - 60.

9. *Ibid.*, p. 60.

10. For an enlightening discussion of the increasing disillusionment of the members of the Scriblerus circle, see Louis I. Bredvold, "The Gloom of the Tory Satirists," *Pope and His Contemporaries: Essays Presented to George Sherburn*, ed. James L. Clifford and Louis A. Landa (Oxford: Clarendon Press, 1949), pp. 1 - 19.

11. *Memoirs*, p. 91. All references to the text of the *Memoirs* are to Kerby-Miller's edition and will be cited internally.

12. *Memoirs*, pp. 193 - 97 *passim*. Kerby-Miller's notes are excellent and copious. Also very helpful, though not easily available, is the second volume of Robert Allen Erickson's *A Critical Edition of the Satires of John Arbuthnot*, 2 vols. (Unpublished Ph.D. dissertation, Yale University, 1967).

13. For the satirical allusions to Woodward, see Kerby-Miller, pp. 206 - 207; for Arbuthnot's relationship with Woodward, see Beattie, pp. 190 - 262 *passim*.

14. Other Scriblerian attacks upon Ambrose Philips are discussed by Kerby-Miller, pp. 220 - 21.

15. *Memoirs*, pp. 243 - 61 passim.

16. *Ibid.*, pp. 272 - 77 *passim*.

17. *Ibid.*, pp. 281 - 93 *passim*.

18. As Kerby-Miller believes (p. 308), the Scriblerians may have received help from William Fortescue, an eminent judge and lawyer, in developing the satire on law.

19. *Ibid.*, p. 294.

20. Richard Owen Cambridge (1707 - 1802), *The Scribleriad: An Heroic Poem* (London: R. Dodsley, 1751).

21. Cibber, *The Refusal*, I, i. See also R. L. Hayley, "The Scriblerians and the South Sea Bubble," *Review of English Studies*, n.s. XXIV (1973), 452 - 58.

22. Three excellent works on the controversy over science and the theory of progress are Anne Burlingame, *The Battle of the Books in its Historical Setting* (New York, 1920), J. B. Bury, *The Idea of Progress* (London, 1924), and Richard Foster Jones, *Ancients and Moderns: A Study of the Scientific Movement in Seventeenth-Century England*, 2nd ed. (St. Louis, 1961).

Chapter Five

1. See, for example, Allardyce Nicoll, *A History of the English Drama, 1660 - 1900*, 3rd ed. (Cambridge: Cambridge University Press, 1955), II, p. 213: "Judged fairly, it is seen to have not a little merit, but its coarseness is certainly unworthy of the hands of the three great *littérateurs* who brought it into being; one might have expected more from such a triumvirate"; or Aitken, p. 89: "*Three Hours after Marriage* deservedly failed." More balanced treatments are to be found in Beattie, pp. 229 - 38; Malcolm Goldstein, *Pope and the Augustan Stage* (Stanford: Stanford University Press, 1958), pp. 22 - 31; the introductions to the Morton-Peterson and Smith editions (see below); George Sherburn, "The Fortunes and Misfortunes of *Three Hours after Marriage*," *Modern Philology*, XXIV (1926), 91 - 109; and Leo Hughes, *A Century of English Farce* (Princeton: Princeton University Press, 1956), pp. 249 - 52.

2. Richard Morton and William M. Peterson, eds., *Three Hours after Marriage*, Lake Erie Studies, Volume I (Painesville, Ohio: Lake Erie College Press, 1961), pp. iii - v. Another text of the play is available in John Harrington Smith's facsimile edition (with introduction) published by the Augustan Reprint Society, Publication Number 91 - 92 (Los Angeles: William Andrews Clark Memorial Library, 1961). Morton and Peterson use the 1717 edition (in its original three-act format) as the basis for their text; Smith reprints the 1758 Dublin edition, which is in five acts.

3. John Wilson Bowyer, *The Celebrated Mrs. Centlivre* (Durham, North Carolina: Duke University Press, 1952), pp. 194 - 206; Sherburn, pp. 95 - 97; Hughes, p. 251.

4. Richard Reynolds, "*Three Hours after Marriage*: Love on Stage," *Eighteenth-Century Life*, I:i (September 1974), 19 - 20.

5. Morton and Peterson, eds., pp. ii - iii. *Three Hours after Marriage* appears to have been the first incident in the long quarrel between Pope and Cibber which went on until just a few months before Pope's death in 1744.

6. Morton and Peterson, eds., pp. 17 - 18.

7. *Ibid.*, p. 18.

8. Simon Trussler, ed., *Burlesque Plays of the Eighteenth Century* (London: Oxford Univeristy Press, 1969), p. 92.

9. Morton and Peterson, eds., p. x.

10. Sherburn, pp. 91 - 92, provides a chronology of the reaction to the play by the authors' contemporaries.

11. Beattie, p. 230; Aitken, p. 90.

12. *A Tale of a Tub*, ed. A. C. Guthkelch and D. Nichol Smith, 2nd edition (Oxford: Clarendon Press, 1958), pp. 250 - 51.

13. *Virgilius Restauratus* has been edited by James Sutherland in *The Dunciad*, Volume V (3rd edition) of Pope's *Poems* (Twickenham Edition), pp. 217 - 21.

14. *Ibid.*, p. 128.

15. *A Tale of a Tub*, ed. Guthkelch and Smith, pp. 95, 103.

16. *Memoirs*, ed. Kerby-Miller, p. 129.

17. Aitken, p. 391. All quotations from the Ginglicutt treatise are from this edition and will be cited in the text.

18. Swift, *Correspondence*, III, p. 439.

19. *Ibid.*

20. *Ibid.*, p. 510.

21. Beattie, p. 228.

22. Joseph Spence, *Anecdotes, Observations, and Characters of Books and Men*, ed. Samuel Weller Singer, 2nd edition (London: John Russell Smith, 1858), p. 152.

23. Aitken, p. 361. All internal citations are to this text.

Chapter Six

1. As quoted in Aitken, p. 55.

2. Beattie, p. 335.

3. "A Supplement" to *The Miscellaneous Works of the Late Dr. Arbuthnot. The Second Volume*, 2nd edition, with additions (Glasgow: James Carlile, 1751), p. 29. All references to *Of the Laws of Chance* (entitled *Of the Hazards of Game* in the 1751 edition) are to this text.

4. Aitken, p. 409. All references to the essay on mathematics are to this text.

5. As quoted in Beattie, p. 339.

6. As quoted in Beattie, p. 340.

7. Beattie, p. 342. Contemporary reactions to Arbuthnot's *Argument* are discussed on pp. 342 - 46.

8. Beattie, p. 209.

9. John W. Clarke and Thomas M. Hughes, *The Life and Letters of the Reverend Adam Sedgwick* (Cambridge: Cambridge University Press, 1890), I, p. 179.

10. J. E. B. Mayor, *Cambridge under Queen Anne* (Cambridge: Deighton, Bell, and Co., 1911), as quoted in Beattie, p. 210.

11. Arbuthnot, *The Miscellaneous Works* (1751 edition), II, pp. 197 -

201. All references to the *Examination* are to this edition and will be cited internally.

12. Beattie, p. 348.

13. *Ibid.*, pp. 348 50.

14. As quoted in Beattie, p. 350.

15. As quoted in Beattie, p. 350.

16. As quoted in Beattie, p. 360.

17. As quoted in Beattie, p. 360.

18. Beattie, pp. 367 - 68.

19. Charles Creighton, *A History of Epidemics in Britain* (Cambridge: Cambridge University Press, 1894), II, p. 403.

20. As quoted in Beattie, p. 372.

21. Beattie, pp. 372 - 75.

Chapter Seven

1. Beattie, pp. 307 - 17.

2. John Gay, *Poetry and Prose*, ed. Vinton A. Dearing and Charles E. Beckwith (Oxford: Clarendon Press, 1975), I, pp. 93 - 94.

3. John Boyle, fifth Earl of Orrery, *Remarks on the Life and Writings of Dr. Jonathan Swift* (London: A. Millar, 1752), Letter XX, pp. 237 - 38.

4. William Cowper, *Correspondence*, ed. Thomas Wright (New York, 1904; reprinted New York: AMS Press, 1968), II, p. 180.

5. Cowper, "Table Talk," *Cowper: Poetical Works*, ed. H. S. Milford, 4th edition with corrections and additions by Norma Russell (London: Oxford University Press, 1967), pp. 14 - 15.

6. George Sherburn, *A Literary History of England*, ed. Albert C. Baugh (New York: Appleton-Century-Crofts, 1948), p. 849.

7. Hugh Walker, *English Satire and Satirists* (London: J. M. Dent; New York: E. P. Dutton, 1925), pp. 197 - 98.

8. Aitken, p. 436. All references to the poem are to this edition and will be cited internally.

9. The manuscript version, which is also reprinted in Aitken, pp. 439 - 42, is preserved in the British Museum and has many variants.

10. Beattie, p. 377.

11. *Ibid.*, pp. 380 - 82.

12. Pope, *Poems* (Twickenham edition), III: i, pp. 53 - 55.

13. *Ibid.*, 166.

14. Thackeray, *Henry Esmond* (Boston: Houghton Mifflin, 1889), p. 438; "Prior, Gay, and Pope" in *The Four Georges; The English Humorists; Sketches and Travels in London* (Boston: Houghton Mifflin, 1889), pp. 254 - 55.

Selected Bibliography

PRIMARY SOURCES

1. Individual Works

An Appendix to John Bull Still in His Senses: or, Law is a Bottomless-Pit. London: John Morphew, 1712. Second, third, and fourth editions were published by Morphew in the same year.
"An Argument for Divine Providence, taken from the constant regularity observed in the Births of both Sexes," *Philosophical Transactions,* XXVII (1710), 186.
A Brief Account of Mr. John Ginglicutt's Treatise concerning the Altercation or Scolding of the Ancients. London: J. Roberts, 1731.
"An Epitaph on Frances Chartres," *The London Magazine* (April 1732). See also *The Gentleman's Magazine* for the same month.
An Essay Concerning the Effects of Air on Human Bodies. London: J. Tonson, 1733. Tonson's firm published another edition in 1751.
An Essay Concerning the Nature of Aliments, and the choice of them, according to the different Constitutions of Human Bodies. London: J. Tonson, 1731. A second edition, *To Which is added, Practical Rules of Diet in the various Constitutions and Diseases of Human Bodies,* was published by Tonson in two volumes in 1732. Other editions by Tonson and his successors appeared in 1735, 1736, 1751, and 1756; another, printed by George Risk, came out in 1731.
An Essay of the Learned Martinus Scriblerus, Concerning the Origin of Sciences. Written to the Most Learned Dr._____F. R. S., from the Deserts of Nubia, in volume III of *Miscellanies in Prose and Verse* (of Pope and Swift). London: Charles Bathurst, 1732.
An Essay on the Usefulness of Mathematical Learning, in a Letter from a Gentleman in the City to His Friend in Oxford. Oxford: Anthony Peisley, 1701. A second edition was published at Oxford in 1721 and a third at London in 1745.
An Examination of Dr. Woodward's Account of the Deluge. London: C. Bateman, 1697.
ΓΝΑΘΙ ΣΕΑΥΤΟΝ *Know Yourself. A Poem.* London: J. Tonson, 1734.
The History of John Bull, in volume II of the Pope-Swift *Miscellanies in Prose and Verse.* London: Benjamin Motte, 1727. Other editions appeared at Edinburgh in 1712 and Glasgow in 1766.

137

————, in *An English Garner,* ed. Edward Arber (London: E. Arber, 1883), VI, 537 - 656.

————, in *Cassell's National Library.* Volume 204. Ed. Henry Morley. London: Cassell, 1889.

————. Ed. Herman Teerink. Amsterdam: H. J. Paris, 1925.

————. Ed. Alan W. Bower and Robert A. Erickson. Oxford: Clarendon Press, 1976. The definitive edition.

————, in *A Miscellany of the Wits.* The Scholar's Library, No. 2. Ed. K. N. Colville. London: Philip Alan, 1920.

John Bull in His Senses. London: J. Morphew, 1712. The second, third, and fourth editions, all printed by Morphew, also appeared in 1712 at London. Another edition was printed at Edinburgh in the same year.

John Bull Still in His Senses. London: J. Morphew, 1712. Morphew also printed the second and third editions in 1712.

Law is a Bottomless-Pit. London: J. Morphew, 1712. The second through the sixth editions, also in 1712, were printed by Morphew, and an edition also appeared at Edinburgh in the same year.

————. Menston, Yorkshire, England: The Scolar Press, 1970.

Lewis Baboon turned Honest, and John Bull Politician. London: J. Morphew, 1712. Morphew's second edition saw print the same year, as did another at Edinburgh.

The Memoirs of Martinus Scriblerus, in *The Works of Mr. Alexander Pope, In Prose, Vol. II.* London: J. and P. Knapton, C. Bathurst, and R. Dodsley, 1741. For other Pope and Swift editions containing the *Memoirs,* see Kerby-Miller's edition (below), pp. 78 - 84.

————. Ed. Charles Kerby-Miller. New Haven: Yale University Press, 1950; New York: Russell and Russell, 1966. This admirable edition is the standard, with a long and very useful introduction and excellent notes.

Of the Laws of Chance. London: Benjamin Motte, 1692.

Oratio Anniversaria Harvaeana. London: J. Tonson, 1727.

Proposals for printing a very Curious Discourse, in Two Volumes in Quarto, Intitled ΨΕΥΔΟΛΟΓΙΑ ΠΟΛΙΤΙΚΗ *or A Treatise of the Art of Political Lying, with an Abstract of the First Volume of the said Treatise.* London: J. Morphew, 1712. Morphew printed a second edition in 1712, and there was another at Edinburgh in the same year.

Reasons humbly offer'd by the Company exercising the Trade and Mystery of Upholders. London: J. Roberts, 1724.

A Sermon preach'd to the People at the Mercat-Cross of Edinburgh on the Subject of the Union. Edinburgh: (?), 1706. Another edition was printed by A. Bell at London in 1707.

Tables of Ancient Coins, Weights and Measures, explain'd and exemplify'd in several Dissertations. London: J. Tonson, 1727.

————. 2nd edition. "To which is added an Appendix . . . by Benjamin

Langwith, D. D." London: D. Browne, A.Millar, J. Whiston, and B. White, 1754.

Tables of the Grecian, Roman and Jewish Measures, Weights and Coins; reduc'd to the English Standard. London: Ralph Smith, 1705.

Three Hours after Marriage. A Comedy. By John Gay. London: Bernard Lintot, 1717. Arbuthnot collaborated on this play with Gay and Pope.

————, in *Burlesque Plays of the Eighteenth Century,* ed. Simon Trussler (London: Oxford University Press, 1969) pp. 91 - 142. Trussler calls the play "an efficient and actable farce, its interest deriving from an ingenious plot, and from characters whose obsession with sex is humorous, in the Jonsonian sense, rather than lascivious."

————. Lake Erie College Studies, Volume I. Ed. Richard Morton and William M. Peterson. Painesville, Ohio: Lake Erie College Press, 1961. The best edition.

————. Augustan Reprint Society Publication No. 91 - 92. Ed. John Harrington Smith. Los Angeles: William Andrews Clark Memorial Library, UCLA, 1961. A facsimile text.

To the Right Honourable The Mayor and Aldermen of the City of London: The Humble Petition of the Colliers, Cooks, Cook-Maids, Blacksmiths, Jack-makers, Brasiers, and others. London: J. Roberts, 1716.

Virgilius Restauratus: seu Martini Scribleri Summi Critici Castigationum in Aeneidum Specimen, in *The Dunciad Variorum.* London: A. Dodd, 1729.

————, in *The Dunciad.* The Twickenham Edition of *The Poems of Alexander Pope,* general editor John Butt. 3rd edition. Ed. James Sutherland. London: Methuen; New Haven: Yale University Press, 1963. Volume V, pp. 217 - 21.

2. Collected Editions

Arbuthnotiana. Augustan Reprint Society Publication No. 154. Ed. Patricia Köster. Los Angeles: William Andrews Clark Memorial Library, UCLA, 1972. Includes *A Catalogue of Dr. Arbuthnot's Library* (1779), listing books belonging to George Arbuthnot and others, and *The Story of the St. Albans Ghost* (1712), which is of doubtful authorship.

A Critical Edition of the Satires of John Arbuthnot. Ed. Robert Allen Erickson. 2 vols. Unpublished Ph.D. dissertation, Yale University, 1967. Volume I contains the texts of nine satires, several of them doubtfully Arbuthnot's, and Volume II is devoted to notes. Included are *The History of John Bull, The Art of Political Lying, The Humble Petition, Reasons Humbly Offer'd, John Ginglicutt's Treatise, Essay Concerning the Origin of the Sciences,* "An Epitaph on Frances Chartres," and the dubious *It Cannot Rain but It Pours* and *Annus Mirabilis.*

The Miscellaneous Works of the Late Dr. Arbuthnot. 2 vols. Glasgow:

James Carlile, 1751. This and the other two collected editions which follow are incomplete; they contain, together with some pieces not by Arbuthnot, the Ginglicutt treatise, the essay on mathematical learning, the examination of Dr. Woodward's account, "Know Yourself," the essay on the laws of chance, and the Mercat-Cross sermon.

————. 2nd edition, with additions. 2 vols. Glasgow: James Carlile, 1751. Shortly after the publication of this edition, George Arbuthnot, the doctor's son, advertised in several papers that this edition was "an imposition on the Publick," probably because it was published without the younger Arbuthnot's permission.

————. A new edition. 2 vols. London: W. Richardson, L. Urquhart, and J. Knox, 1770. Contains a brief biographical sketch of Arbuthnot.

3. Letters

Ross, Angus, ed. *The Correspondence of Dr. John Arbuthnot.* Unpublished Ph. D. dissertation, Cambridge University, 1956. Contains about 200 letters from and to Arbuthnot as well as extensive commentary and analysis.

Sherburn, George, ed. *The Correspondence of Alexander Pope.* 5 vols. Oxford: Clarendon Press, 1956. Includes many letters between Pope and Arbuthnot.

Williams, Harold, ed. *The Correspondence of Jonathan Swift.* 5 vols. Oxford: Clarendon Press, 1963 - 1965. Contains numerous letters between Swift and Arbuthnot.

SECONDARY SOURCES

1. Books

Aitken, George A. *The Life and Works of John Arbuthnot.* Oxford: Clarendon Press, 1892; New York: Russell and Russell, 1968. Still useful, this book has an outdated bibliography, genealogical notes, and an anthology of the authentic and doubtful works of Arbuthnot.

Beattie, Lester M. *John Arbuthnot, Mathematician and Satirist.* Cambridge: Harvard University Press, 1935; New York: Russell and Russell, 1968. A full and excellent critical biography, this book examines Arbuthnot's work in far greater detail than does Aitken's.

Bruneteau, Claude. *John Arbuthnot (1667 - 1735) et les ideés au debut du dix-huitième siècle.* Lille: Universite de Lille III, Service de reproduction des theses, 1974. 2 volumes. A very long (949 pages) doctoral dissertation dealing with Arbuthnot's career, his writings on domestic and foreign affairs, and his moral philosophy.

[Hilles, F. W.] *Johnson on Dr. Arbuthnot.* Privately printed, 1957. A small pamphlet describing Dr. Johnson's alterations in paragraphs 212 - 13 of his life of Pope.

Passon, Richard Henry. *The Satiric Art of Dr. John Arbuthnot.* Unpublished Ph.D. dissertation, Notre Dame University, 1965; abstracted in *Dissertation Abstracts,* XXVI (1966), 5416. Analyzes Arbuthnot's major satires in terms of their dominant theme of man's philosophic pride in his own nature.

SESSOMS, HENRY M. *The Art of Scriblerian Prose Satire.* Unpublished Ph.D. dissertation, Vanderbilt University, 1968; abstracted in *Dissertation Abstracts,* XXIX (1969), 2282A. Places Scriblerian satire in the tradition of Menippean prose satire and analyzes the techniques of Pope, Swift, Arbuthnot, Gay, and Parnell in their collaborative writings.

WEIDENBRONER, STEPHEN S. *The Influence of John Arbuthnot on the Scientific Attitudes Expressed by Pope, Swift, and the Scriblerus Club.* Unpublished Ph.D. dissertation, New York University, 1969; abstracted in *Dissertation Abstracts International,* XXX (1970), 3440A. Discusses the individual attitudes of Arbuthnot, Pope, and Swift (and other Scriblerians) toward the emergence of the new science.

2. Articles

AITKEN, GEORGE A. "Dr. Arbuthnot," *Athenaeum,* 17 June 1893, p. 766. Deals with minor facts regarding Arbuthnot's parentage, sixteenth-century ancestors, and medical education.

————. "Arbuthnot's Brothers," *Athenaeum,* 18 June 1892, pp. 792 - 93. Provides additional information about George and Robert Arbuthnot.

BEATTIE, LESTER M. "The Authorship of *The Quidnuncki's,*" *Modern Philology,* XXX (1933), 317 - 20. Demonstrates, on the basis of two letters from Dr. William Stratford to Edward Harley on February 4 and 10, 1734, that Arbuthnot is the poem's probable author.

COOKE, ALICE L. "The Shadow of Martinus Scriblerus in Hawthorne's 'The Prophetic Pictures,' " *New England Quarterly,* XVII (1944), 597 - 604. Hawthorne's story may have been influenced by *The Memoirs of Martinus Scriblerus;* both deal with the theme of the absurdity of impractical knowledge.

D[ENNIS], J[OHN]. "John Arbuthnot," *Cornhill Magazine,* XXXIX (1879), 91 - 101. Quotes Pope, Swift, Johnson, and Chesterfield in praise of Arbuthnot, provides a brief biography, and comments upon various aspects of Arbuthnot's work.

ERICKSON, ROBERT A. "Situations of Identity in the *Memoirs of Martinus Scriblerus,*" *Modern Language Quarterly,* XXVI (1965), 388 - 400. Explores the criticism of certain philosophic notions and the definition of human nature.

FERGUSON, DELANCEY. "Arbuthnot, John," *Encyclopedia Americana,* 1975 ed., II, 181. A brief essay.

FREEHAFER, JOHN. "Arbuthnot and the Dublin Pirates," *The Scriblerian,* II (1970), 65 - 67. The current state of Arbuthnot's bibliography is neither full nor usable; there were at least twenty-one printings of his work in Dublin before 1735, not just nine, as previously thought.

HAYLEY, R. L. "The Scriblerians and the South Sea Bubble," *Review of English Studies*, n.s. XXIV (1973), 452 - 58. In Colley Cibber's *The Refusal* (1721), I, i, Dr. Bullanbear is probably Arbuthnot, while other characters represent Pope, Gay, and Swift.

"John Arbuthnot, M.D., Died February 27, 1735," *Times Literary Supplement*, 28 February 1935, pp. 113 - 14. A sensitive and perceptive essay about Arbuthnot on the bicentennial of his death.

JN. C. [JOHN CHALKER]. "Arbuthnot, John," *Encyclopaedia Britannica*, 1971 ed., II, 222. A brief biography.

KIPPIS, ANDREW. *Biographica Britannica*. London: C. Bathurst, 1778, volume I. One of the earliest biographies.

KNOEPFLMACHER, U. C. "The Poet as Physician: Pope's Epistle to Dr. Arbuthnot," *Modern Language Quarterly*, XXXI (1970), 440 - 49. Arbuthnot serves as a straight man who complements Pope's own self-characterization.

KÖSTER, PATRICIA. "Arbuthnot's Use of Quotation and Parody in His Account of the Sacheverell Affair," *Philological Quarterly*, XLVIII (1969), 201 - 11. Relates the political and religious troubles of Dr. Henry Sacheverell to the allegory of the John Bull pamphlets.

———. "Swift, Arbuthnot, and the Law," *American Notes and Queries*, IV:6 (February 1969), 83 - 84. Comments upon the satire on law in *Gulliver's Travels* and *The History of John Bull*.

LEWIS, PETER E. "Dramatic Burlesque in *Three Hours after Marriage*," *Durham University Journal*, XXXIII (1972), 232 - 39. Discusses the play as a burlesque of Augustan comedy and dramatic poetry.

M., E. F. "Dr. Edmund Halley," *Notes and Queries*, CLXXXIX, (1945), 105. Discusses a letter to Arbuthnot by the astronomer on May 6, 1711, relating to the Flamsteed controversy.

MCKILLOP, ALAN DUGALD. "The Geographical Chapter in Scriblerus," *Modern Language Notes*, LXVIII (1953), 480 - 81. Bernhardus Varenius's *Geographia Generalis* (1650) may be the main source for Chapter II of *The Memoirs of Martinus Scriblerus*.

MAYO, THOMAS F. "The Authorship of the History of John Bull," *PMLA*, XLV (1930), 274 - 82. Attacks Herman Teerink's ascription of the work to Swift.

MICHAEL, WOLFGANG. "Who Is John Bull?" *Contemporary Review*, CXLIV (1933), 314 - 19. Accepts Arbuthnot as the author of the John Bull pamphlets and argues that John Bull is Henry St. John, Viscount Bolingbroke.

MOSSNER, ERNEST CAMPBELL. "Hume's Epistle to Dr. Arbuthnot, 1734: The Biographical Significance," *Huntington Library Quarterly*, VII (1944), 135 - 52. An unaddressed letter by David Hume, often called the "Letter to a Physician," is probably to Arbuthnot.

PASSON, RICHARD H. "Legal Satire in *Gulliver* from *John Bull*," *American Notes and Queries*, V (1967), 99 - 100. The satire on the English legal system in Book IV, Chapter 5, of *Gulliver's Travels* seems to echo a passage in *John Bull Still in His Senses.*

POTTER, GEORGE R. "Swift and Natural Science," *Philological Quarterly,* XX (1941), 97 - 118. Touches briefly upon Swift's relationship to Arbuthnot in their satires on science.

REYNOLDS, RICHARD. "*Three Hours after Marriage:* Love on Stage," *Eighteenth-Century Life,* I:1 (September 1974), 19 - 20. The play is part of a "paper war" by the three authors against John Dennis and Charles Gildon.

RICHARDSON, BENJAMIN WARD. "John Arbuthnot, M.D., F.R.S., The Medical Scholar," *Aesclepiad,* IV (1887), 142 - 71. Reprinted in Richardson's *Disciples of Aesculapius* (London: Hutchinson, 1900), I, 205 - 26. A survey of Arbuthnot's medical career, with some attention to the essay concerning the effects of air.

ROSS, ANGUS. "Notes on the Letters of Dr. Arbuthnot," *The Scriblerian,* II (1969), 1 - 2. Arbuthnot's letters show a disregard for standard writing practice with their erratic punctuation and capitalization, a lack of self-consciousness, and his refusal to hide traces of his Scottish background.

SHERBURN, GEORGE. "The Fortunes and Misfortunes of *Three Hours after Marriage,*" *Modern Philology,* XXIV (1926), 91 - 109. A critical examination of the play and a discussion of the reasons for its failure.

SHUMATA, NATSUO. "John Arbuthnot," *Eigo Seinen* (Tokyo), CXVIII (1972), 88 - 89. In Japanese.

SIMPSON, A. A. L. "The Originator of John Bull," *London Mercury,* XIX (1928), 69 - 78. An appreciative biographical sketch.

SUTHERLAND, JAMES R. "Pope or Arbuthnot?" *Times Literary Supplement,* 22 November 1935, p. 770. A prose pamphlet, "Annus Mirabilis" (1722), is probably by neither writer.

WALKER, HUGH. *English Satire and Satirists* (London: J. M. Dent; New York: E. P. Dutton, 1925), pp. 197 - 202. Suggests that, among the English prose satirists, Arbuthnot was "nearly equal" to Swift "in native gifts, and incomparably more amiable and attractive."

Index